MW01448246

شَرْحُ وَصِيَّةِ الْإِمَامِ ابْنِ الْقَيِّمِ لِنَفْسِهِ وَلِسَائِرِ إِخْوَانِهِ مِنْ أَهْلِ السُّنَّةِ فِي وجُوب نُصْرَةِ الحَقّ

IBN AL QAYYIM'S ADVICE TO AHL AL-SUNNAH CONCERNING THE OBLIGATION OF

SUPPORTING THE TRUTH

From the *Nūniyyah* Poem
(*al Kāfiyah al-Shāfiyah fi-l Intiṣār lil Firqa al-Nājiyah*)

With detailed explanatory notes from:
Aḥmad bin 'Isā al-Najdī (1253-1327 h.)
Abd al-Raḥmān bin Nāṣir al-Sa'dī (1307-1376 h.)
Muḥammad Khalīl Harrās (1334-1395 h.)
Muḥammad bin Ṣāliḥ al 'Uthaymīn (1347-1421 h.)
Ṣāliḥ bin Fawzān al Fawzān

al Jawziyyah, Ibn al Qayyim.
(contributor) al-Najdī, Aḥmad bin 'Isā.
(contributor) al-Sa'dī, Abd al-Raḥmān bin Nāṣir.
(contributor) Harrās, Muḥammad Khalīl.
(contributor) al 'Uthaymīn, Muḥammad bin Ṣāliḥ.
(contributor) al Fawzān, Ṣāliḥ bin Fawzān
(translator) Quinn, Umar.

First Printing, 2018.
Explanation of Ibn al Qayyim's Advice to the Himself and His Brothers from Ahl al-Sunnah [From the Nuniyyah Poem]
ISBN: 9781729252000
1. Nonfiction > Religion > Islam > General
2. Nonfiction > Religion > Islam > Rituals and Practice

www.SalafiCulture.com
Salaficulture@gmail.com

شَرْحُ وَصِيَّةِ الإِمَامِ ابْنِ الْقَيِّمِ لِنَفْسِهِ وَلِسَائِرِ إِخْوَانِهِ مِنْ أَهْلِ السُّنَّة في
وجُوب نُصْرَةِ الحَقّ

IBN AL QAYYIM'S ADVICE TO AHL AL-SUNNAH CONCERNING THE OBLIGATION OF

SUPPORTING THE TRUTH

From the Nūniyyah Poem
(*al Kāfiyah al-Shāfiyah fi-l Intiṣār lil Firqa al-Nājiyah*)

With detailed explanatory notes from:
Aḥmad bin 'Isā al-Najdī (1253-1327 h.)
Abd al-Raḥmān bin Nāṣir al-Sa'dī (1307-1376 h.)
Muḥammad Khalīl Harrās (1334-1395 h.)
Muḥammad bin Ṣāliḥ al 'Uthaymīn (1347-1421 h.)
Ṣāliḥ bin Fawzān al Fawzān (1354 h. -)

Translated & Compiled by:
Abū Suhailah 'Umar Quinn

Table of Contents

Table of Contents

Table of Contents 5
Arabic Ligatures & Transliteration Guide 9
The Importance of Ibn al Qayyim's Advice 11
Arabic Text of the Advice with English Translation 27
I. Introductory Advices 43
Synopsis of Lines 1-6 45
1. Sincerely Wanting Salvation 47
2. Hold Fast to the Waḥiyy 49
3. Support the Book & the Sunnah 50
4. Strike the People of Falsehood with the Truth 51
5. Determination 55
6. Firmness & Patience 56
II. Brandishing the Weapon of Truth 61
Synopsis of Lines 7-13 63
7. Brandishing the Sword of Truth 64
8. Having Audacity against Falsehood 66
9. & 10. Proclaim the Truth, Even with Few Supporters; Allah Aids the Religion 67
11. The Reality of their Plots 69
12. Angels vs. Devils 70
13. Contrast the Two Sides 72
III. How to Overcome the People of Falsehood 73
Synopsis of Lines 14-20 75
14. Victory comes with Patience 76
15. Remember the Past 76
16. Use the Texts Against Them 78
17. Do Not Be Intimidated by Their Numbers 79
18. Preoccupy Them with Each Other 81
19. Do Not Fear Their Advance 83
20. Wait for Adequate Support 85
IV. Necessary Qualities for Victory 89

Synopsis of Lines 21-27 91
21. Strength in Unity 93
22. Do Not be Helpless, Complain or Be Fearful 94
23. Ridding Oneself of Loathsome Traits 95
24. Compound Ignorance & Blind Fanaticism 95
25. Objectivity & Fairness 101
26. Fearing Allah & Genuineness for the Messenger 103
27. Hold Fast & Place Your Trust in Allah 104

V. The Description of the Truth 107

Synopsis of Lines 28-33 109
28. The Truth is an Attribute of Allah and He Alone Guides to It 111
29. Allah is Upon the Straight Path of Truth 114
30. The Truth is Victorious & Trialled 116
31. Trialling Distinguishes Allah's Allies from His Enemies 119
32. You Win Some, You Lose Some 121
33. The Final Outcome will Always Favor the Righteous 122

VI. The Two Migrations 127

Synopsis of Lines 34-39 129
34. Two Mandatory Migrations 130
35. The First Migration: Sincerity 133
36. The Definition of Sincerity 133
37. Sincerity Spares a Person from Shirk 135
38: Migration to the Prophet (ﷺ) 135
39. The Reality of The Second Migration 136

VII. Restricting Arbitration to Two Judges 139

Synopsis of Lines 40-46 141
40. Men's Statements are to be Weighed Against the Revelation 142
41. & 42. The Revelation is the Source of All Justice, & it is the Cure & Guide 144
43. The Sunnah is the Second Arbiter 148
44. The Reality of Everything Besides These Two Judges 149
45. & 46. No Honor or Cooperation with the People of Falsehood 150

VIII. The True Cause of Victory 153

Synopsis of Lines 47-51 155
47. & 48. The Futility of the Opposition 156
49. Righteous Deeds: The Best Means of Victory 157
50. Victory is Not by Numerical Superiority 159
51. How the Ṣaḥāba (رضي الله عنهم) Conquered the Hearts 162

IX. The Reality of Courage 163

Synopsis of Lines 52-58 165
52. The First Type of Courage 167
53. The Second Type of Courage 168
54. What Happens When These Two Combine? 173
55. Selecting Well-Matched Opponents 174
56. - 58. Experienced Advice About People 176

X. Beautiful Patience, Clemency, and Ostracizing 181

Synopsis of Lines 59-63 183
59. Reiteration of Boldness & Fearlessness 184
60. Sincere Boycotting 185
61. Beautiful Patience & Beautiful Clemency 186
62. Beautiful Ostracizing 188
63. The Preordainment of Guidance & Misguidance 191

XI. Looking at People from Two Perspectives 193

Synopsis of Lines 64-68 195
64. & 65. Having a Balance Outlook at People 196
66. The Second Perspective 197
67. & 68. Weeping out of Fearfulness of Allah 205

XII. Concluding Advice 213

Synopsis of Lines 69-73 215
69. Beware of Your Inner-Flaws 216
70. The Harm of Vindictiveness 220
71. The Divine Promise of Victory 222
72. Allah Recompenses People Accordingly 224
73. Who This Advice is Written For 224

Appendix: al-Sa'dī's Summarization of Ibn al Qayyim's Advice. 227

Arabic Ligatures & Transliteration Guide:

b	=	ب	z	=	ز	f	=	ف
t	=	ت	s	=	س	q	=	ق
th	=	ث	sh	=	ش	k	=	ك
j	=	ج	ṣ	=	ص	l	=	ل
ḥ	=	ح	ḍ	=	ض	m	=	م
kh	=	خ	ṭ	=	ط	n	=	ن
d	=	د	ẓ	=	ظ	h	=	ه
dh	=	ذ	'	=	ع	w	=	و
r	=	ر	gh	=	غ	y	=	ي

Short: a = َ ; i = ِ ; u = ُ

Long: ā = ا ; ī = ي ; ū = و

Diphthong: ay = اي ; aw = او

The following appear after the mention of Allah:

(عَزَّوَجَلَّ) 'azza wa jalla [Allah, Mighty and Majestic]
(تَبَارَكَ وَتَعَالَىٰ) tabāraka wa ta'ālā [Allah, Blessed and Exalted]
(سُبْحَانَهُ وَتَعَالَىٰ) subḥanahu wa ta'ālā [Allah, glorified and exalted above all imperfection]

The following appear after the mention of the Prophet Muhammad or other Prophets.

(صَلَّى ٱللَّهُ عَلَيْهِ وَسَلَّمَ) ṣallāllahu 'alayhi wa sallam [May Allah raise his mention and grant him peace]
(عَلَيْهِمَا ٱلسَّلَامُ) 'alayhimās-salām [peace be upon them - dual]

(عَلَيْهِمُ السَّلَامُ) 'alayhimus-salām [peace be upon them]

The following appear after the mention of the Ṣaḥāba:
(رَضِيَ اللَّهُ عَنْهُ) raḍiyullahu 'anhu [may Allah be pleased with him]
(رَضِيَ اللَّهُ عَنْهَا) raḍiyullahu 'anhā [may Allah be pleased with her]
(رَضِيَ اللَّهُ عَنْهُمَا) raḍiyallahu 'anhumā [may Allah be pleased with them — dual]
(رَضِيَ اللَّهُ عَنْهُمْ) raḍiyallahu 'anhum [may Allah be pleased with them]

The following appear after the mention of righteous Muslims:

(رَحِمَهُ اللَّهُ) raḥimahullah [may Allah show him mercy]
(رَحِمَهُمُ اللَّهُ) raḥimahumullah [may Allah show them mercy]
(حَفِظَهُ الله) ḥafiẓahullah [may Allah preserve/protect him]

The Importance of Ibn al Qayyim's Advice

The Importance of Ibn al Qayyim's Advice

The Subject Matter of the Nūniyyah

Supporting the truth and its triumphing over falsehood is the overall subject of *Ibn al Qayyim's* lengthy poem *al Kāfiyah al-Shāfiyah fī-l intiṣār lil Firqa al-Nājiyah* [That Which Suffices and Remedies as Pertains the Triumphing of the Saved Sect], as is evident from its very name. The poem is most commonly called the *Nūniyyah* because every verse of poetry is concluded with the Arabic consonant "*nūn*." The *Nūniyah* itself consists of 5,842 lines of poetry, making it quite a remarkable, one-of-a-kind work in *'aqīdah*. The great scholar al-Sa'dī says about its exceptionality:

> (It) includes that which is not found in any other single book on the topic of monotheism, beliefs, and fundamentals. It contains details that are not found in other books, including the writings of the author himself.[1]

In the *Nūniyyah*, the author of the poem systematically defends the *'aqīdah* of *Ahl al-Sunnah* by repudiating many groups of deviation who had plagued Muslim society for centuries and had caused it to reach an unprecedented point of crisis. In this and many other writings he fully elaborates on this crisis and the unmistakable cause of it. For example, in one instance he said:

> In summary, the splitting of the people of the previous two scriptures, and the splitting of this nation into seventy-three

[1] al-Tawḍīḥ al Mubīn li Tawḥīd al Anbiyā' wal Mursalīn, p. 11. Dār 'Aalam al Fawā'id; 1st edition, 1420.

> sects was caused by misinterpretation. The blood of Muslims was only ever shed...because of misinterpretation. The enemies of Islām, such as the philosophers, the *Qirāmiṭah*, the *Bāṭiniyyah*, the *Ismā'iliyyah*, and the *Nuṣayriyyah*, only infiltrated through the door of misinterpretation. Islām has never been trialled with any tribulation except on account of misinterpretation. Such tribulation transpired either: by way of the misinterpreters themselves; or by way of the unbelievers being unleashed against them. This was on account of what they had perpetrated of misinterpretation, what they opposed of the obvious meaning of revealed religion, and what they had justified of false reasoning.[2]

So defending the creed of the Sunnah against misinterpretation and misrepresentation constitutes the first line of defense for the religion as a whole. If beliefs about Allah (عَزَّوَجَلَّ) are open to reinterpretation, then what would remain off limits thereafter? As such, elsewhere, Ibn al Qayyim explains the inherent danger of reinterpreting the Divine Attributes of the Creator saying:

> Applying this (false) principle (i.e., the admissibility of reinterpreting the Divine Attributes) would necessarily allow for the reinterpretation of the verses pertaining divine commandment and prohibition, those pertaining divine promise and threat, and those pertaining divine reward and punishment. We have mentioned in the book *al Ṣawā'iq al Mursalah* that misinterpretation of the verses and narrations pertaining the divine attributes in a manner that removes them away from their literal meanings constitutes the foundational cause of the corruption of the world and the

2 'Ilām al Muwaqi'īn 'an Rabbil 'Alamīn vol. 4, p. 193. Dar al Kutub al 'Ilmiyyah Beirut (1411).

> religion, and that of the departure of kingdoms. It was only by way of misinterpretation that the enemies of Islām gained control over them. Those who have investigated and are experienced pertaining what has happened in the world know this well. Accordingly, some intelligent people from the philosophers forbid reinterpretation, despite them believing it to be correct, because it is the cause of the corruption of the world and discarding of religious matters.

Likewise, Ibn al Qayyim's most formative mentor, Shaykh al Islām Ibn Taymiyyah (رَحِمَهُ ٱللَّهُ) outlined the seriousness of this historical threat, saying that:

> Those who are familiar with the events of history unanimously agree that the worst sword unsheathed upon *ahl al qiblah* (i.e. the Muslims) was from those who ascribing to it; and that the greatest corruption that transpired against the Muslims who ascribe to the *qibla* came exclusively from those sects affiliated to them. They are the most extreme in harming the religion and its people.[3]

Because Ibn al Qayyim (رَحِمَهُ ٱللَّهُ) keenly understood the nature of the threat presented by deviant doctrines that are antithetical to the core tenets of Islamic creed, he reiterates the dire importance of supporting the truth and repudiating falsehood throughout his writings. He says in the beginning pages of the *Qaṣīda al-Nūniyyah*, before commencing with the poem itself:

> *Jihād* (lit. struggling) by means of evidence and explanation is assigned primacy to *jihād* conducted by way of sword and weaponry. That is why (Allah), in the Meccan *surahs* commanded that it be conducted as a notification and

[3] Majmū al Fatāwā vol. 28, p. 479.

forewarning (of impending divine punishment) at a time and place where there was no *jihād* by way of the hand. Allah (تَبَارَكَ وَتَعَالَىٰ) said:

﴿ فَلَا تُطِعِ الْكَافِرِينَ وَجَاهِدْهُم بِهِ جِهَادًا كَبِيرًا ﴾

"So do not obey the disbelievers, and strive against them with the Qur'an a great striving." [al Furqān: 52]

Also, Allah commanded to make jihād against the *munāfiqīn* (i.e., the hypocrites) and to be stern with them despite their coexistence with the Muslims in both residency and travel. (Allah) (تَبَارَكَ وَتَعَالَىٰ) said:

﴿ يَا أَيُّهَا النَّبِيُّ جَاهِدِ الْكُفَّارَ وَالْمُنَافِقِينَ وَاغْلُظْ عَلَيْهِمْ ﴾

"Strive hard against the disbelievers and the hypocrites." [al-Tawbah: 73]

So *jihād* by way of knowledge and evidence is the *jihād* of Allah's Prophets and Messengers (عَلَيْهِمُ السَّلَامُ), and it is that of the most elite of His worshipful servants who were specially designated to be recipients of guidance, providence, and unity. Whoever dies without battling or inwardly desiring to do so, then he dies upon a branch of hypocrisy.

It is enough for a servant to be ascribed with blindness and desertion who sees the contingents of faith and the forces of the *Sunnah* and *Qurān* having strapped on their armor for combat and readied their equipment, positioning in formation and standing in their designated locations, reaching a fevered pitch while the gears of combat churn and individual contenders summon each other to duel — all while he is sequestered behind a safe haven and in grottoes. If fate drives him to exit therefrom, then he might do as much as sit on the hill with the spectators, watching to see who wins this time around so that he can join their ranks. Thereupon he goes to them swearing by Allah with his most ardent oath saying: "I was with you all the while and was wishing for your lot to be the victors."

It is only rightful for someone who has self-respect and self-worth not to sell himself for the vilest price and not to subject himself to instances of degradation and indignity tomorrow when he stands in front of Allah (عَزَّوَجَلَّ) and the Messenger (صَلَّاللَّهُعَلَيْهِوَسَلَّمَ). He is to firmly plant his feet alongside the ranks of the people of knowledge and faith and not to align himself with any doctrine besides that which has come in the *Sunnah* and the *Qurān*.

It is as though the veil has already been removed and as though the dust has settled, revealing the faces of Ahl al-Sunnah to be radiant, smiling, and rejoicing at good news, whereas the faces of Ahl al Bida' are dust-stained and covered with darkness.

﴿ يَوْمَ تَبْيَضُّ وُجُوهٌ وَتَسْوَدُّ وُجُوهٌ ﴾

"On the Day (i.e. the Day of Resurrection) when some faces will become white and some faces will become black." [Aal 'Imrān: 106]

Ibn 'Abbās said: The faces of the adherents of Sunnah and unity will be brightened, whereas the faces of the proponents of religious innovation and division will be darkened.

So by Allah! It is easier to separate from the proponents of whimsicalities and innovations in this world than accompanying them at the point when it is said:

﴿ احْشُرُوا الَّذِينَ ظَلَمُوا وَأَزْوَاجَهُمْ ﴾

"Assemble those who did wrong, together with their companions." [al-Ṣāfāt: 22]

The chief of the believers, 'Umar bin al Khaṭṭāb (رَضِيَ ٱللَّهُ عَنْهُ) said: "Their azwāj means those that they resemble and their counterparts." Also, Allah (عَزَّوَجَلَّ) said:

﴿ وَإِذَا النُّفُوسُ زُوِّجَتْ ﴾

"And when the souls are paired." [al-Takwīr: 7].

So the person of truth will accompany his counterpart that is at his level while the person of falsehood will accompany his counterpart that is at his level. By Allah, at that point the oppressor will bite upon his hands, once the reality of what he achieved in this world comes to bear upon him.

﴿ وَيَوْمَ يَعَضُّ الظَّالِمُ عَلَىٰ يَدَيْهِ يَقُولُ يَا لَيْتَنِي اتَّخَذْتُ مَعَ الرَّسُولِ سَبِيلًا (27) يَا وَيْلَتَىٰ لَيْتَنِي لَمْ أَتَّخِذْ فُلَانًا خَلِيلًا (28) لَّقَدْ أَضَلَّنِي عَنِ الذِّكْرِ بَعْدَ إِذْ جَاءَنِي ۗ وَكَانَ الشَّيْطَانُ لِلْإِنسَانِ خَذُولًا (29) ﴾

"And the Day the wrongdoer will bite on his hands [in regret] he will say, 'Oh, I wish I had taken with the Messenger a way. Oh, woe to me! I wish I had not taken that one as a friend. He led me away from the remembrance after it had come to me. And ever is Satan, to man, a deserter.'" [al Furqān: 27-29][4]

Ibn al Qayyim's Sincere Advice to Himself & His Brothers

In keeping with the overall recurrent theme of defending the Sunnah that is the cornerstone of this famous poem, then in the hands of the respected reader is a translation of an indispensable advice entailed therein. This particular advice is

---

4 See *al Kāfiyah al-Shāfiyah fī-l Intiṣār lil Firqah al-Nājiyah*, pp. 10-12; Dār 'Aalam al Fawā'id lil nashr wa-l-tawzī'; 1st Edition 1428.

about the obligation of supporting and defending the truth. It outlines the pertinent qualities and manners requisite for that task, as is located within an introductory chapter of the *Nūniyah* Poem. This specific chapter commences with line number 188:

يَا أَيُّهَا الرَّجُلُ المُرِيدُ نَجَاتَهُ ... اسْمَعْ مَقَالَةَ نَاصِحٍ مِعْوَانِ

"Oh man who desires his own salvation: Listen to the statement of a sincere advisor and helper."

It concludes with Ibn al Qayyim's statement on line number 260:

هَذِي وَصِيَّةُ نَاصِحٍ وِلِنَفْسِهِ ... وَصَّى وَبَعْدُ لِسَائِرِ الإِخْوَانِ

"This is an advice from someone sincere — it is offered in introspection and then it is for all brethren."

Thus, the text of this specific chapter comprises 73 lines of poetry that bear the subtitle: "*faṣl: fī muqaddimatin nāfi'ah qablat-taḥkīm*" [i.e., pertaining a beneficial preliminary word before arbitration]. The text of this advice is further accompanied by a detailed scholarly synopsis and annotation from six separate authoritative sources.

al-Shaykh Muḥammad bin Ṣāliḥ al 'Uthaymīn (رَحِمَهُ ٱللَّهُ) says about the important advices found in this introductory chapter of the *Nūniyyah*:

> In reality, these are guidelines. If while encountering these advices you recorded, took note of them and then transferred them to a specified notebook, it would prove to be of a great benefit and reference source for you. That is

> because these are guidelines that you won't find anywhere except in this book.[5]

Likewise, the renowned Egyptian scholar, Muḥammad Khalīl Harrās remarked on the preciousness of Ibn al Qayyim's advice. He said:

> After the author finishes mentioning Jahm's corrupt doctrines and what he had drowned in of misguidance — on account of having and aversion to the texts and relegating them to misinterpretation — he then proceeds with these invaluable advices for whoever is adamant on achieving salvation from Allah's torment — with which He threatened every stray renegade.

In his commentary of select passages from the *Nūniyyah*, the great scholar 'Abd al-Raḥmān bin Nāṣir al-Sa'dī (رَحِمَهُ ٱللَّهُ) characterizes this preliminary advice as follows:

> At this point he [i.e., Ibn al Qayyim (رَحِمَهُ ٱللَّهُ)] commences in a beneficial introduction and comprehensive advice that every student of knowledge is in need of, regardless of whether [his studies] pertain knowledge of the Usūl (primary tenets) or knowledge of the Furū' (subsequent rulings). Furthermore, it is befitting to being assigned precedence over [studying] the etiquette of the scholar and the student. This is because it entails pieces of advices needed by every person desiring felicity in both worlds.[6]

The Structure of this Book

This present work combines the explanations of five great scholars whose synopsis and annotations of the *Nūniyyah* are

---

[5] *Sharḥ al Kāfiya al-Shāfiyah.*

[6] *Tawḍīḥ al Kāfiya al-Shāfiya*

the best known and most widely referenced. In chronological order, these scholars and their commentaries are as follows:

(1.) Aḥmad bin 'Isā al-Najdī (رَحِمَهُ ٱللَّهُ) (1253-1327 h.) whose explanation is titled: *Tawḍīḥ al Maqāṣid wa Taṣḥīḥ al Qawā'id fī Sharḥ Qaṣīda al Imām ibn al Qayyim.*

(2.) 'Abd al-Raḥmān bin Nāṣir al-Sa'dī (رَحِمَهُ ٱللَّهُ) (1307-1376 h.), who wrote multiple commentaries on the *Nūniyyah* such as: [a.] *Tawḍīḥ al Kāfiyah al Shāfiyah*, which is a synopsis of the entire poem without quoting the text of the *Qaṣīdah* for brevity's sake. He explains the entire *Nūniyyah* except for the lengthy concluding description of Paradise. Al-Sa'dī was of the view that Ibn al Qayyim's book *Ḥādī al Arwāḥ ilā Bilād al Afrāḥ* about Paradise sufficed as an explanation on the subject. The section that is relevant to the advice explained in the present book is included as a concluding appendix to summarize the greater meanings of the 73 lines of poetry. [b.] Furthermore, Al-Sa'dī wrote two extensive explanations, of varying lengths, for the chapter titled the Monotheism of the Prophets and Messengers (عَلَيْهِمُ ٱلسَّلَامُ). The first and shorter of these is titled: *Al Ḥaqq al Wāḍiḥ al Mubīn fī Tawḥīd al Anbiyā wal Mursalīn.* The second is titled: *Al Tawḍīḥ al Mubīn li Tawḥīd al Anbiyā' wal Mursalīn.* Both are published in Arabic in multiple printings and editions. [c.] Al-Sa'dī also wrote an explanation for select passages from the Nūniyah that is titled: *al-Ta'līqāt al-Sa'dīyyah 'alā Qiṭa'h min Nūniyyah ibn al Qayyim wal 'Aqīdah al-Safārīniyyah.* This brief, yet beneficial, commentary of al-Sa'dī is available throughout the present book.

(3.) Muḥammad Khalīl Harrās (رَحِمَهُ ٱللَّهُ) (1334-1395 h.) whose explanation is simply titled: *Sharḥ Qaṣīdah al-Nūniyah.* His method of explanation is perhaps the most unique in as much as that he divides the poetry into individual thematic segments and then comments on each, as opposed to commenting on select lines or passages or explaining it line by line, as is commonplace in most explanations of the *Nūniyyah*.

(4.) Muḥammad bin Ṣāliḥ al 'Uthaymīn (رَحِمَهُ ٱللَّهُ) (1347-1421 h.) whose four volume explanation is titled: *Sharḥ al Kāfiya al-Shāfiyah.* It is the lengthiest existent explanation of the *Nūniyyah* and was transcribed from audio recordings of two separate explanations of the *Nūniyyah*, the second of which is more detailed. The first recorded explanation was originally from regular classes conducted at his masjid in 'Unayzah between the years 1408-1412 *hijrī*. Having given his permission to transcribe and publish this explanation, he later wished to provide a more detailed explanation. So in the year 1419 h., following the example of his Shaykh al-Sa'dī (رَحِمَهُ ٱللَّهُ), Ibn 'Uthaymīn (رَحِمَهُ ٱللَّهُ) focused greater attention on *The Monotheism of the Prophets and Messengers* (عَلَيْهِمُ ٱلسَّلَامُ), initiating his second, more detailed commentary, beginning with the prefatory lesson to that section. Chronologically, these chapters occur towards the end of the *Nūniyyah*; and so, after explaining the subsequent chapters until the conclusion of the poem, he then commenced in reexplaining the *Nūniyyah* in greater detail from its beginning, He succeeded in providing a more detailed explanation for much of the poem, ultimately reaching line 1177 before his death in 1421.

(5.) The renowned senior scholar, Ṣāliḥ bin Fawzān al Fawzān (حفظه الله) whose commentary is simply titled *al-Ta'līq al Mukhtaṣar 'alā Nūniyyah Ibn al Qayyim*.

Three of these five contributors represent a succession of direct scholarly tutelage: Aḥmad bin Ibrāhīm bin 'Īsā al-Najdī

(رَحِمَهُ ٱللَّهُ) was one of the many *shuyūkh* of al-Sa'dī. Al-Sa'dī (رَحِمَهُ ٱللَّهُ), in turn, was the most impactful teacher and mentor of al-Shaykh Muḥammad bin Ṣāliḥ al 'Uthaymīn (رَحِمَهُ ٱللَّهُ). The renowned scholar Ṣāliḥ bin Fawzān al Fawzān (حفظه الله) also undoubtedly hails from a long line of scholars who generationally taught and explained this masterful text.

Another contributor, Muḥammad Khalīl Harrās (رَحِمَهُ ٱللَّهُ) was famously preparing his Azhar University dissertation as an attempted repudiation against Ibn Taymiyyah's critiques of the Ash'arīs and philosophers. In the course of his research, he was guided to adopting the creed and methodology of the Salaf, thereafter teaching and authoring in its defense until his last days. His invaluable and exceptional explanation of the *Nūniyyah* serves as one of the most profound examples of that blessed legacy.

These five scholars took different approaches to the study of the *Nūniyah*. Muḥammad Khalīl Harrās has the most unique approach which was that he segments the poetry into passages divided according to subject matter, after which he provides a summary synopsis of each respective passage. His segmenting of passages has been replicated in this present book, and his synopsis of each passage is the first commentary provided in the sequential order of each section. Harrās's synopsis is then followed by brief explanatory notes of Ibn 'Isā, al-Sa'dī, and al Fawzān, each of whom have commented on certain select passages of the Nūniyah. Ibn 'Uthaymīn (رَحِمَهُ ٱللَّهُ) has provided the most detailed explanation of each line, which representing the longest of the five explanations, and so his comments are placed last in order. As an appendix to these five explanations, this book concludes with a summarization and overview of the entire chapter that was written by al-Sa'dī (رَحِمَهُ ٱللَّهُ) in the book *Tawḍīḥ al Kāfiyah al-Shāfiyah.*

Additionally, these seventy-three lines of poetry have been grouped into twelve segments, comprising the main subjects of the chapter, according to the selection of Muḥammad Khalīl Harrās in his synopsis. Each segment has been assigned individual subject headings that are representative of the main theme of the respective segment. Most lines have also been assigned sub-topic headings. This is done in hopes of improving readability and providing greater accessibility to the meanings of the text.

Important Note on Terms Referring to Fighting & Jihād in this Book

As is evident from the text of the *Nūniyyah,* its explanations, and other similar writings, the import of terminologies denoting fighting and *jihād,* as intended in this poem, are in reference to the subject matter of the etiquette of scholarly debate, supporting the truth, and repudiation of falsehood. The broader subject matter of supporting and the defending the truth according to one's capacity is the concern of every Muslim. In the conclusion of the *Nūniyyah*, Ibn al Qayyim (رَحِمَهُ ٱللَّهُ) says:

هَذَا وَنَصْرُ الدِّينِ فَرْضٌ لَازِمٌ ... لاَ لِلْكِفَايَةِ بَلْ عَلَى الْأَعْيَانِ

"Along with this, supporting the religion is a binding obligation — not communal in nature but rather it is upon each individual."

بِيَدٍ وَإِمَّا بِاللِّسَانِ فَإِنْ عَجَزْ ... تَ فَبِالتَّوَجُّهِ وَالدُّعَا بِجِنَانِ

"It is done by way of the hand or the tongue, yet if you are unable, then it is done by having avid interest and heartfelt supplication."

مَا بَعْدُ ذَا وَاللهِ لِلْإِيْمَانِ حَبَّـ ... ـةُ خَرْدَلٍ يَا نَاصِرَ الإِيْمَانِ

"Beyond that, by Allah, there is not a mustard seed of faith remaining, O supporter of the faith!"

As for the he broader rulings, prerequisites, and etiquettes of matters pertaining international relations, war and peace, and similar sensitive topics, then that is the domain of the most erudite *'Ulemā* and the prerogative of those charged with authority in Muslim lands. Those subjects are thoroughly discussed in classical books of Islamic *siyāsah* [i.e., politics],[7] jurisprudence and collections of authoritative scholarly edicts. It is certainly not left to the fanciful, grandiose preoccupation of reckless youth, or other commoners and laity. Islam is a religion of wisdom and timeliness. As this poem reminds us, patience and composure is the key to victory.

To reiterate this point, the following is an indispensable advice from the great scholar Muḥammad bin Ṣāliḥ al 'Uthaymīn (رَحِمَهُ ٱللَّهُ) pertaining how to wisely respond to abusiveness and belligerence when in a situation of weakness and vulnerability:

> It is mandatory upon a person to react to the abuse that is perpetrated by the unbelievers by employing patience, seeking heavenly reward, and waiting for relief. One should not imagine that the situation will end quickly and easily. Allah (تَبَارَكَ وَتَعَالَىٰ) may test believers with unbelievers who harm and possibly kill them, just as they killed Prophets (عَلَيْهِمُ ٱلسَّلَامُ) — just as the Tribe of Israel, the Jews, killed some of the Prophets, who are far greater than the preachers and Muslims at large. So one is to be patient, wait for deliverance, and

7 Such as *al Aḥkām al-Sulṭāniyah* of al Mawridī, *al Aḥkām al-Sulṭāniyah* of al Qāḍī Abū Ya'lā, and *al-Siyāsa al-Shari'yyah* of Ibn Taymiyyah.

not get fed-up or upset. Rather, he is to stand tall and be like the boulder, in as much as that the ultimate outcome is in favor of the pious, and Allah is with the patient. A person is patient and persistent, pursuing the paths that lead to the objective. However, one is to do so without chaos, and without recruiting or instigating! Alternatively, they must have an orderly method. This is because the enemies of the Muslims from the hypocrites and disbelievers are following a stable, orderly plan and are attaining their objective.

As for the shallow-minded who get carried away by emotions until they rise up and recruit, then they may miss out on a great deal of good. Perhaps they commit an error that ruins all that they have built — if they have even built anything. However, the believer is to be patient, staying ready, and behaving deliberately while developing himself and coming up with an organized plan to forego any harm from Allah's enemies from the hypocrites and disbelievers and to deprive them of any opportunity, because they are waiting for opportunities to overcome the people of goodness. They want to antagonize them, so that some of them do something that justify their (enemies) placing themselves above them while saying this is exactly what we want. Great evil would happen as a result.

The Prophet (صَلَّى ٱللَّٰهُ عَلَيْهِ وَسَلَّمَ) told people before you to exercise patience, while patience is more applicable to you. A person would implement this and remain patient. So you, O *Ummah* of Muḥammad (صَلَّى ٱللَّٰهُ عَلَيْهِ وَسَلَّمَ), are a nation of patience and kindness. Be patient until Allah (عَزَّ وَجَلَّ) brings forth His command, and the ultimate outcome will favor the pious. You, as an individual, are not to be silent against evil but rather act in an organized fashion, having a plan and employing good dealings. Wait for Allah's relief and do not get fed-up, do not get fed-up. This phase is long, especially in the beginning of the tribulation, because those responsible for it are trying their utmost to reach the pinnacle of what they want. So you are to cut the path off from them, have more stamina than them and be more powerful than them in planning. Because these adversaries are plotting and Allah (عَزَّوَجَلَّ) is plotting and He is the best of plotters. And Allah is the Granter of success.[8]

[8] Sharḥ Riyāḍ al-Ṣāliḥīn vol. 1, p. 252-254.

Arabic Text of Poetry with English Translation

فَصْل: فِي مُقَدِّمَةٍ نَافِعَةٍ قَبْلَ التَّحْكِيم

A Beneficial Preliminary Advice Before Issuing Judgment

يَا أَيُّهَا الرَّجُلُ المُرِيدُ نَجَاتَهُ ... اسْمَعْ مَقَالَةَ نَاصِحٍ مِعْوَانِ

[1. /(188.)] Oh man who desires his own salvation: Listen to the statement of a sincere advisor and helper.

كُنْ فِي أُمُورِكَ كُلِّهَا مُتَمَسِّكاً ... بِالوَحْيِ لاَ بِزَخَارِفِ الهَذَيَانِ

[2./(189.)] In all of your matters be one who holds fast to the revelation and not to that of ornamented babble.

وَانْصُرْ كِتَابَ اللهِ والسُّنَنَ الَّتِي ... جَاءَتْ عَنِ المَبْعُوثِ بِالفُرْقَانِ

[3./(190.)] Support Allah's Book and those Sunan that have come from the one who was dispatched with the Criterion.

وَاضْرِبْ بِسَيْفِ الوَحْيِ كُلَّ مُعَطِّلٍ ... ضَرْبَ المُجَاهِدِ فَوْقَ كُلِّ بَنَانِ

[4./(191.)] And strike down every mu'aṭṭl [i.e., negator] with the sword of the revelation — with the blow of a Mujāhid against every joint.

وَاحْمِلْ بِعَزْمِ الصِّدْقِ حَمْلَةَ مُخْلِصٍ ... مُتَجَرِّدٍ لِلَّهِ غَيْرِ جَبَانِ

[5./(192.)] And bear against them with genuine determination — with the advancing of someone sincere — devotedly for Allah, not being a coward.

وَاثْبُتْ بِصَبْرِكَ تَحْتَ أَلْوِيَةِ الهُدَى ... فَإِذَا أُصِبْتَ فَفِي رِضَا الرَّحْمَنِ

[6./(193.)] Be firm in your patience under the standards of guidance. So that when you are struck, then that will be within Allah's Good-Pleasure.

وَاجْعَلْ كِتَابَ اللهِ وَالسُّنَنَ الَّتِي ... ثَبَتَتْ سِلَاحَكَ ثُمَّ صِح بِجَنَانِ

[7./(194.)] Make as your weapon Allah's Book and those Sunan that are authentically established, and then scream with all of your heart:

مَنْ ذَا يُبَارِزْ فَلْيُقَدِّمْ نَفْسَهُ ... أَوْ مَنْ يُسَابِقْ يَبْدُ فِي المَيْدَانِ

[8./(195.)] Who wants to contend? Then let him bring himself forward! Who wants to race forward? Then let him step onto the field!

وَاصْدَعْ بِمَا قَالَ الرَّسُولُ وَلَا تَخَفْ ... مِنْ قِلَّةِ الأَنْصَارِ وَالأَعْوَانِ

[9./(196.)] Boldly proclaim what the Messenger (صَلَّى ٱللَّهُ عَلَيْهِ وَسَلَّمَ) said and do not be fearful from having few supporters and helpers.

فَاللهُ نَاصِرُ دِينِهِ وَكِتَابِهِ ... وَاللهُ كَافٍ عَبْدَهُ بِأَمَانِ

[10./(197.)] Allah is the Aider of His religion and His Book. And Allah is the Sufficer for His worshipper by way of protection.

لَا تَخْشَ مِنْ كَيْدِ العَدُوِّ وَمَكْرِهِمْ ... فَقِتَالُهُمْ بِالْكِذْبِ وَالبُهْتَانِ

[11.] Do not fear the plot of the enemy and their conspiring. For indeed they fight by means of lying and slander.

فَجُنُودُ أَتْبَاعِ الرَّسُولِ مَلَائِكٌ ... وَجُنُودُهُمْ فَعَسَاكِرُ الشَّيْطَانِ

[12./(199.)] The armies of the Messenger's followers are angels, whereas their armies [i.e., the people of falsehood] are the troops of Satan.

شَتَّانَ بَيْنَ العَسْكَرَيْنِ فَمَنْ يَكُنْ ... مُتَحَيِّراً فَلْيَنْظُرِ الفِئَتَانِ

[13. /(200.)] How great is the difference between the two armies! So whoever wants to pick a side then let him contrast the two parties.

وَاثْبُتْ وَقَاتِلْ تَحْتَ رَايَاتِ الهُدَى ... وَاصْبِرْ فَنَصْرُ اللهِ رَبِّكَ دَانِ

[14. /(201.)] Be firm and fight under the banners of guidance (i.e., defend the truth and repudiate falsehood). And be patient, for indeed the help of Allah, your Lord, is near.

وَاذْكُرْ مَقَاتِلَهُمْ لِفُرْسَانِ الهُدَى ... لِلَّهِ دَرُّ مَقَاتِلِ الفُرْسَانِ

[15. /(202.)] Mention their fatal flaws to the cavalry of guidance, How commendable is it to tell the cavalry where to strike!

وَادْرَأْ بِلَفْظِ النَّصِّ فِي نَحْرِ العِدَا ... وَارْجُمْهُمْ بِثَوَاقِبِ الشُّهْبَانِ

[16. /(203.)] Push back with the wordings of the texts in front of the adversary, and shoot at them with rapid balls of fire.

لاَ تَخْشَ كَثْرَتَهُمْ فَهُمْ هَمَجُ الوَرَى ... وَذُبَابُهُ أَتَخَافُ مِنْ ذِبَّانِ

[17.] Do not fear their numbers, for they are the rabble and flies of creation. Or are you afraid of flies?

وَاشْغَلْهُمْ عِنْدَ الجِدَالِ بِبَعْضِهِمْ ... بَعْضاً فَذَاكَ الحَزْمُ لِلْفُرْسَانِ

[18. /(205.)] When debating them, preoccupy them with each other. That affords resoluteness to the horsemen.

وَإِذَا هُمْ حَمَلُوا عَلَيْكَ فَلَا تَكُنْ ... فَزِعاً لِحَمْلَتِهِمْ وَلَا بِجَبَانِ

[19. /(206.)] And when they bear down upon you then do not be frightened at their offense and do not be a coward.

وَاثْبُتْ وَلَا تَحْمِلْ بِلاَ جُنْدٍ فَمَا ... هَذَا بِمَحْمُودٍ لَدَى الشُّجْعَانِ

[20. /(207.)] Be firm and do not launch an offense without an army for that is not commendable in the estimation of the brave.

فَإِذَا رَأَيْتَ عِصَابَةَ الإِسْلَامِ قَدْ ... وَافَتْ عَسَاكِرُهَا مَعَ السُّلْطَانِ

[21. /(208.)] So when you see the faction of Islam have assembled with their regiments alongside the Sulṭān,

فَهُنَاكَ فَاخْتَرِقِ الصُّفُوفَ وَلَا تَكُنْ ... بِالعَاجِزِ الوَانِي وَلَا الفَزْعَانِ

[22. /(209.)] Then at that point penetrate the ranks and do not be the one who is helpless weakling and do not be terrified.

وَتَعَرَّ مِنْ ثَوْبَيْنِ مَنْ يَلْبَسْهُمَا ... يَلْقَى الرَّدَى بِمَذَمَّةٍ وَهَوَانِ

[23. /(210.)]Disrobe of two garments that cause whoever wears them to encounter ruin in dispraise and degradation:

ثَوْبٌ مِنَ الجَهْلِ المُرَكَّبِ فَوْقَهُ ... ثَوْبُ التَّعَصُّبِ بِئْسَتِ الثَّوْبَانِ

[24. /(211.)] A garment of compound ignorance above which is a garment of blind-fanaticism, how terrible are these two garments!

وَتَحَلَّ بِالإِنْصَافِ أَفْخَرَ حُلَّةٍ ... زِيْنَتْ بِهَا الأَعْطَافُ وَالْكَتِفَانِ

[25. /(212.)] Adorn yourself with objectivity, which is the most respectable apparel used to beautify the sides and shoulders.

وَاجْعَلْ شِعَارَكَ خَشْيَةَ الرَّحْمَنِ مَعْ ... نُصْحِ الرَّسُولِ فَحَبَّذَا الأَمْرَانِ

[26. /(213.)] Make your shi'ār [lit. Slogan, emblem, or immediate clothing] the fear of al-Raḥmān along with genuineness for the Messenger, how commendable are these two matters!

وَتَمَسَّكَنَّ بِحَبْلِهِ وَبِوَحْيِهِ ... وَتَوَكَّلَنَّ حَقِيقَةَ التُّكْلَانِ

[27. /(214.)] And hold fast to his rope and his revelation, and place your reliance on Him with true dependency.

فَالحَقُّ وَصْفُ الرَّبِّ وَهْوَ صِرَاطُهُ الـ ... هَادِي إِلَيْهِ لِصَاحِبِ الإِيْمَانِ

[28. /(215.)] For al Ḥaqq is a description of al-Rabb and it is His path guiding to Him for the possessor of faith.

وَهُوَ الصِّرَاطُ عَلَيْهِ رَبُّ العَرْشِ أَيْـ ... ضاً، ذَا وَذَا قَدْ جَاءَ فِي القُرْآنِ

[29. /(216.)] It is also the path that the Lord of the throne is upon — both this and that have come in the Qurān.

وَالحَقُّ مَنْصُورٌ وَمُمْتَحَنٌ فَلَا ... تَعْجَبْ فَهَذِي سُنَّةُ الرَّحْمَنِ

[30. /(217.)] The truth is aided and trialled so do not be amazed, for this is the way of al-Raḥmān.

وَبِذَاكَ يَظْهَرُ حِزْبُهُ مِنْ حَرْبِهِ ... وَلِأَجْلِ ذَاكَ النَّاسُ طَائِفَتَانِ

[31. /(218.)] By that His ḥizb becomes distinct from those warring with Him. And for that reason people are of two parties.

وَلِأَجْلِ ذَاكَ الحَرْبُ بَيْنَ الرُّسْلِ وَالْـ ... كُفَّارِ مُذْ قَامَ الوَرَى سَجْلَانِ

[32. /(219.)] And on account of that و *warring transpired between the Messengers and the unbelievers since humankind's beginning, alternating very much (between victory and defeat).*

لَكِنَّمَا العُقْبَى لِأَهْلِ الحَقِّ إِنْ ... فَاتَتْ هُنَا كَانَ لَدَى الدَّيَّانِ

[33. /(220.)] However, the final outcome will favor the people of truth. And if that does not happen here then it will happen upon meeting with al Dayyān [i.e., Allah, the Divine Judge].

وَاجْعَل لِقَلْبِكَ هِجْرَتَيْنِ وَلَا تَنَمْ ... فَهُمَا عَلَى كُلِّ امْرِئٍ فَرْضَانِ

[34. /(221.)] Make your heart embark upon two migrations and do not sleep. For certainly they are mandatory for every person.

فَالهِجْرَةِ الأُوْلَى إِلَى الرَّحْمَنِ بِالْـ ... إِخْلَاصِ فِي سِرٍّ وَفِي إِعْلَانِ

[35. /(222.)] The first is the migration to al-Raḥmān by way of sincerity in private and in public.

فَالْقَصْدُ وَجْهُ اللهِ بِالْأَقْوَالِ وَالْ ... أَعْمَالِ وَالطَّاعَاتِ وَالشُّكْرَانِ

[36. /(223.)] So the intention is to be for Allah's Face, by words and deeds, acts of obedience and gratitude.

فَبِذَاكَ يَنْجُو العَبْدُ مِنْ إِشْرَاكِهِ ... وَيَصِيرُ حَقًّا عَابِدَ الرَّحْمَنِ

[37. /(224.)] By doing that, the worshipful-slave is spared from ascribing partners to him, and in doing so truly becomes a worshipful-slave for al-Raḥmān.

والهِجْرَةُ الأُخْرَى إِلَى الْمَبْعُوثِ بِالْـ ... حَقِّ المُبِينِ وَوَاضِحِ البُرْهَانِ

[38. /(225.)] The other migration is to the one who was dispatched with the unambiguous truth and clear proof.

فَيَدُورُ مَعَ قَوْلِ الرَّسُولِ وَفِعْلِهِ ... نَفْيًا وَإِثْبَاتًا بِلَا رَوَغَانِ

[39. /(226.)] So he operates in accordance to the Messenger's statements and actions pertaining what is negated and what is affirmed, without any shiftiness.

وَيُحَكِّمُ الوَحْيَ المُبِينَ عَلَى الَّذِي ... قَالَ الشُّيوُخُ فَعِنْدَهُ حَكَمَانِ

[40. /(227.)] He arbitrates with the unambiguous revelation over what was said by Shuyūkh. Therefore, he only has two matters by which to judge.

لاَ يَحْكُمَانِ بِبَاطِلٍ أَبَداً وَكُلُّ ... العَدْلِ قَدْ جَاءَتْ بِهِ الحَكَمَانِ

[41. /(228.)] Neither of them ever judge in falsehood, rather every justice has been brought by these two judges.

وَهُمَا كِتَابُ اللهِ أَعْدَلُ حَاكِمٍ ... فِيهِ الشِّفَا وَهِدَايَةُ الحَيْرَانِ

[42. /(229.)] These are: Allah's book, which is the fairest arbiter, entailing the cure and guidance for the bewildered.

والحَاكِمِ الثَّانِي كَلَامُ رَسُولِهِ ... مَا ثَمَّ غَيْرُهُمَا لِذِي إِيْمَانِ

[43. /(230.)] And the second judge is the Messenger's speech. There is none other besides these two for the person of faith.

فَإِذَا دَعَوْكَ لِغَيْرِ حُكْمِهِمَا فَلَا ... سَمْعًا لِدَاعِي الْكُفْرِ وَالعِصْيَانِ

[44. /(231.)] If they invite you to anything other than the judgement of these two, then do not listen to one inviting to disbelief and disobedience.

قُلْ لَا كَرَامَةَ لا، ولا نُعْمَى وَلَا ... طَوْعاً لِمَنْ يَدْعُو إِلَى طُغْيَانِ

[45. /(232.)] Say: no honor, no satisfaction and no cooperation for one inviting to transgression.

وَإِذَا دُعِيتَ إِلَى الرَّسُولِ فَقُلْ لَهُمْ ... سَمْعًا وَطَوْعًا لَسْتُ ذَا عِصْيَانِ

[46. /(233.)] If you are invited to the Messenger (ﷺ), then say to them: I hear and obey, and I am not from the disobedient.

وَإِذَا تَكَاثَرَتِ الخُصُومُ وَصَيَّحُوا ... فَاثْبُتْ فَصَيْحَتُهُمْ كَمِثْلِ دُخَانِ

[47. /(234.)] When the opponents become many and they scream in commotion, then be firm -- for their screaming is like nothing but smoke.

يَرْقَى إِلَى الأَوْجِ الرَّفِيعِ وَبَعْدَهُ ... يَهْوِي إِلَى قَعْرِ الحَضِيضِ الدَّانِي

[48. /(235.)] It rises up to a high point, after which it blows away to the nearest low surface.

هَذَا وَإِنَّ قِتَالَ حِزْبِ اللهِ بِالْـ ... أَعْمَالِ لاَ بِكَتَائِبِ الشُّجْعَانِ

[49. /(236.)] Additionally, the fighting of Allah's faction is by way of deeds, not by contingents of brave warriors.

وَاللهِ مَا فَتَحُوا البِلَادَ بِكَثْرَةٍ ... أَنَّى وَأَعْدَاءُهُمْ بِلَا حُسْبَانِ

[50. /(237.)] By Allah they did not conquer the land by way of numbers!
How could that be when their enemies were unimaginable?

وَكَذَاكَ مَا فَتَحُوا القُلُوبَ بِهَذِهِ الْـ ... آرَاءِ بَلْ بِالْعِلْمِ وَالإِيمَانِ

[51. /(238.)] Likewise, they did not conquer the hearts by means of these opinions, but rather it was by knowledge and faith.

وَشَجَاعَةُ الفُرْسَانِ نَفْسُ الزُّهْدِ فِي ... نَفْسٍ، وَذَا مَحْذُورُ كُلِّ جَبَانِ

[52. /(239.)] The warrior's courage is none other than zuhd (abstemiousness/disinterestedness) pertaining one's life, whereas that is something from which every coward is deprived.

وَشَجَاعَةُ الحُكَّامِ وَالْعُلَمَاءِ زُهْـ ... ـدٌ فِي الثَّنَا مِنْ كُلِّ ذِي بُطْلَانِ

[53. /(240.)] The courage of the rulers and the scholars is disinterest in the lauding of every person of falsehood.

فَإِذَا هُمَا اجْتَمَعَا لِقَلْبِ صَادِقٍ ... شَدَّتْ رَكَائِبُهُ إِلَى الرَّحْمَنِ

[54. /(241.)] When these two unite within the heart of a person of genuineness, then his steeds will gallop quickly to al-Raḥmān.

وَاقْصِدْ إِلَى الأَقْرَانِ لاَ أَطْرَافِهَا ... فَالْعِزُّ تَحْتَ مَقَاتِلِ الأَقْرَانِ

[55. /(242.)] Seek out the most worthy opponents and not the outer flanks. Honor is found within the skirmishes of worthy opponents.

وَاسْمَعْ نَصِيحَةَ مَنْ لَهُ خُبْرٌ بِمَا ... عِنْدَ الوَرَى مِنْ كَثْرَةِ الجَوَلاَنِ

[56. /(243.)] Listen to the advice of one well-informed of what the people possess due to abundant encounters.

مَا عِنْدَهُمْ وَاللهِ خَيْرٌ غَيْرَ مَا ... أَخَذُوهُ عَمَّنْ جَاءَ بِالْقُرَآنِ

[57. /(244.)] By Allah! They have no good with them save that which they received from the one who came with the Qurān.

والكُلُّ بَعْدُ فَبِدْعَةٌ أَوْ فِرْيَةٌ ... أَوْ بَحْثُ تَشْكِيكٍ وَرَأْيُ فُلاَنِ

[58. /(245.)] Everything else thereafter is innovation, fabrication or skeptical research and the opinionating of fulān [i.e., so-and-so].

فَاصْدَعْ بِأَمْرِ اللهِ لاَ تَخْشَ الوَرَى ... فِي اللهِ وَاخْشَاهُ تَفُزْ بِأَمَانِ

[59. /(246.)] Boldly proclaim your Lord's command and don't fear the people as pertains Allah. But rather fear Him so as to successfully attain safety.

وَاهْجُرْ وَلَوْ كُلَّ الوَرَى فِي ذَاتِهِ ... لاَ فِي هَوَاكَ وَنَخْوَةِ الشَّيْطَانِ

[60. /(247.)] Boycott, if you must, all of the people for His sake. However, do not do so for your own whims or out of the pride caused by Shayṭān.

وَاصْبِرْ بِغَيْرِ تَسَخُّطٍ وَشِكَايَةٍ ... وَاصْفَحْ بِغَيْرِ عِتَابِ مَنْ هُوَ جَانِ

[61. /(248.)] Be patient without being upset and complaining. Overlook without retribution against the offender.

وَاهْجُرْهُمُ الهَجْرَ الجَمِيلَ بِلَا أَذًى ... إِنْ لَمْ يَكُنْ بُدٌّ مِنَ الهِجْرَانِ

[62. /(249.)] Boycott them with beautiful ostracizing, namely, that which is without abusiveness — in the instance where boycotting is unavoidable.

وَانْظُرْ إِلَى الأَقْدَارِ جَارِيَةً بِمَا ... قَدْ شَاءَ مِنْ غَيٍّ وِمِنْ إِيْمَانِ

[63. /(250.)] Look at the preordainments occurring just as He willed pertaining misguidance and faith.

وَاجْعَل لِقَلْبِكَ مُقْلَتَيْنِ كِلَاهُمَا ... بِالحَقِّ فِي ذَا الخَلْقِ نَاظِرَتَانِ

[64. /(251.)] Assign two eyes to your heart, both of which view the creation by means of the truth.

فَانْظُرْ بِعَيْنِ الحُكْمِ وَارْحَمْهُمْ بِهَا ... إِذْ لَا تُرَدُّ مَشِيئَةُ الدَّيَّانِ

[65. /(252.)] Look through the eye at what he preordained and feel mercy towards them thereby, because nothing can refuse the will of al-Dayyān.

وَانْظُر بِعَيْنِ الأَمْرِ وَاحْمِلْهُمْ عَلَى ... أَحْكَامِهِ فَهُمَا إِذَنْ نَظَرَانِ

[66. /(253.)] Also, look with the eye of Divine commandment and bind them to His laws. For these are two different viewpoints.

وَاجْعَلْ لِوَجْهِكَ مُقْلَتَيْنِ كِلَاهُمَا ... مِنْ خَشْيَةِ الرَّحْمَنِ بَاكِيَتَانِ

[67. /(254.)] Make sure that in your face you have two eyes, both of which weep out of fearing al-Raḥmān.

لَوْ شَاءَ رَبُّكَ كُنْتَ أَيْضًا مِثْلَهُمْ ... فَالْقَلْبُ بَيْنَ أَصَابِعِ الرَّحْمَنِ

[68. /(255.)]Had your Lord willed, you would have also been like them, for the hearts are between al-Raḥmān's Fingers.

وَاحْذَرْ كَمَائِنَ نَفْسِكَ اللَاتِي مَتَى ... خَرَجَتْ عَلَيْكَ كُسِرْتَ كَسْرَ مُهَانِ

[69. /(256.)] Be on caution against the innermost facets of your self which are such that if they emerged against you, you'd be broken in degradation.

وَإِذَا انْتَصَرْتَ لَهَا فَأَنْتَ كَمَنْ بَغَى ... طَفْيَ الدُّخَانِ بِمَوْقِدِ النِّيرَانِ

[70. /(257.)] Were you to seek victory/exact retribution on its behalf, then you would be like one trying to extinguish smoke by lighting a fire.

وَاللهُ أَخْبَرَ وَهُوَ أَصْدَقُ قَائِلٍ ... أَنْ سَوْفَ يَنْصُرُ عَبْدَهُ بِأَمَانِ

[71. /(258.)] Allah, who is the speak to speak, has informed that He would aid his worshipper with safety.

مَنْ يَعْمَلِ السُّوآى سَيُجْزَى مِثْلَهَا ... أَوْ يَعْمَلِ الحُسْنَى يَفُزْ بِجِنَانِ

[72. /(259.)] Whoever commits evil will be recompensed its like; and whoever does what is best will successfully attain Paradise.

هَذِي وَصِيَّةُ نَاصِحٍ وِلِنَفْسِهِ ... وَصَّى وَبَعْدُ لِسائِرِ الإِخْوَانِ

[73. /(260.)] This is an advice from someone sincere — it is offered in introspection and then it is for all of his brethren.

Detailed Scholarly Synopsis & Annotation of Ibn al Qayyim's Advice

I. Introductory Advices
Synopsis of Lines 1-6:

1. Sincerely Wanting Salvation

2. Hold Fast to the Waḥiyy

3. Support the Book & the Sunnah

4. Strike the People of Falsehood with the Truth

5. Determination

6. Firmness & Patience

I. Introductory Advices

يَا أَيُّهَا الرَّجُلُ المُرِيدُ نَجَاتَهُ ... اسْمَعْ مَقَالَةَ نَاصِحٍ مِعْوَانِ

[1. /(188.)] Oh man who desires his own salvation: Listen to the statement of a sincere advisor and helper.

كُنْ فِي أُمُورِكَ كُلِّهَا مُتَمَسِّكاً ... بِالوَحْيِ لاَ بِزَخَارِفِ الهَذَيَانِ

[2./(189.)] In all of your matters hold fast to the revelation and not to that of ornamented babble.

وَانْصُر كِتَابَ اللهِ والسُّنَنَ الَّتِي ... جَاءَتْ عَنِ المَبْعُوثِ بِالفُرْقَانِ

[3./(190.)] Support Allah's Book and those Sunan that have come from the one who was dispatched with the Criterion.

وَاضْرِبْ بِسَيْفِ الوَحْيِ كُلَّ مُعَطِّلٍ ... ضَرْبَ المُجَاهِدِ فَوْقَ كُلِّ بَنَانِ

[4./(191.)] And strike down every mu'aṭṭl [i.e., negator] with the sword of the revelation — with the striking of a soldier at every limb and joint.

وَاحْمِلْ بِعَزْمِ الصِّدْقِ حَمْلَةَ مُخْلِصٍ ... مُتَجَرِّدٍ لِلَّهِ غَيْرِ جَبَانِ

[5./(192.)] And bear against them with genuine determination — with the advancing of someone sincere. (Do so) devotedly for Allah, not being a coward.

وَاثْبُتْ بِصَبْرِكَ تَحْتَ أَلْوِيَةِ الهُدَى ... فَإِذَا أُصِبْتَ فَفِي رِضَا الرَّحْمَنِ

[6./(193.)] Be firm in your patience under the banner of guidance. So that when you are struck then that will be within Allah's Good-Pleasure.

Synopsis of Lines 1-6

Muhammad Khalīl Harrās (رَحِمَهُ ٱللَّهُ) summarizes:

After the author finishes mentioning Jahm's corrupt doctrines and what he had drowned in of misguidance — on account of aversion to the texts and relegating them to reinterpretation — he then proceeds with these invaluable advices for whoever seeks salvation from Allah's torment, which is what He has threatened for every stray renegade. So he advises him to hold fast to the clear revelation pertaining all affairs of religiosity, while being averse to the misrepresentation of the people of falsehood. Also, he is to strive to defend Allah's book and the *Sunan* that are reported on the authority of the one whom Allah (عَزَّوَجَلَّ) dispatched with the Criterion. Furthermore, he is to utilize the texts of the two revelations as a sword by which to strike the proponents of *ta'ṭīl* and fabrication, just as the soldier strikes his opponent at every joint. He is to employ genuine determination whilst engaged in his campaign, being sincere to Allah (عَزَّوَجَلَّ) without being timid or shaken. He is also to be resolute under the banner of guidance and faith, without retreating or succumbing to defeat. If he is smitten by anything, then that is within the scope of Allah's good-pleasure, which is an objective for which all altruism and sacrifice is deemed but a small-price and something easy to procure.

فَصْل: في مُقَدِّمَةٍ نَافِعَةٍ قَبْلَ التَّحْكِيم

A Beneficial Preliminary Advice Before Issuing Judgment

'Abd al-Rahmān al-Sa'dī (رحمه الله) explains:

At this point, he engages in a beneficial introduction and comprehensive advice that every student of knowledge is in need of, regardless of whether (his studies) be knowledge of the *usūl* (foundational tenets) or knowledge of the *furū'* (secondary tenets).

Furthermore, it is befitting to being assigned precedence over (learning) the etiquette of the scholar and the student. This is because it entails pieces of advice needed by every person desiring felicity in both worlds.

Muhammad bin Sālih al 'Uthaymīn (رحمه الله) explains:

Having mentioned what he mentioned about the principles of the people of innovation, he then initiates a chapter for arbitration.

So he says: "*Oh man who desires his own salvation: Listen to the statement of a sincere advisor and helper.*"

1. Sincerely Wanting Salvation

يَا أَيُّهَا الرَّجُلُ المُرِيدُ نَجَاتَهُ ... اسْمَعْ مَقَالَةَ نَاصِحٍ مِعْوَانِ

[1. /(188.)] Oh man who desires his own salvation: Listen to the statement of a sincere advisor and helper.

Ahmad bin 'Isā al-Najdī (رحمه الله) explains:

At this point there is a commencement of a beneficial advice and comprehensive introduction before initiating arbitration between the various sects. The author — may Allah (عَزَّوَجَلَّ) sanctify his soul and brighten his grave — issues it as an advice to those who truly understand about Allah. That is owing to the fact that the human being is not created purposeless and uncared for, but rather, Allah (عَزَّوَجَلَّ) has created him for a tremendous matter and (to fulfill) a massive covenant. Allah (عَزَّوَجَلَّ) created him to worship Him, which is a combination of loving and fearing Him while being humble and subservient to Him. He has prepared two worlds: there is a world of good-recompense for good-doers and another world of punishment for the opposers.

So it is imperative for one who seeks personal salvation to ready and prepare himself for that which will bring him closer to his Lords's good-pleasure while sparing him from His punishment and torment. There is no way to do that except by following the Messenger (صَلَّى ٱللَّهُ عَلَيْهِ وَسَلَّمَ) in all that is minor or major, placing obedience to him before obedience to anyone else. For this reason he said: "*Oh man you desires his own salvation*"... until the end [of those lines of poetry]. This is just as the author says later on:

"Oh you who desires his soul's salvation from hell and the blazing flames on the day of reckoning."[9]

The "*M'iwān*" is one who is good at helping or who does so a great deal, as was stated by the author of the *Qāmūs*.

'Abd al-Rahmān al-Sa'dī (رَحِمَهُ ٱللَّهُ) explains:

So he [i.e., Ibn al Qayyim (رَحِمَهُ ٱللَّهُ)] specifies that such a person is one whose intention is to spare himself from punishment in this world and in the hereafter.

Muhammad bin Sālih al 'Uthaymīn (رَحِمَهُ ٱللَّهُ) explains:

Mi'wān has the meaning of *mu'īn* [i.e., helper], but it is more extensive than that in its meaning. So just as helping can be done with actions, then likewise it can be done with statements. So he is addressing the man because the man is the one who should be addressed on account of his awareness of what is to be respected and what is acceptable. His saying "*who*

9 This is an important advice found in a later chapter of Ibn al Qayyim's Nuniyyah titled: *A Lesson Pertaining Identifying that Following the Sunnah and Qurān is the Path of Salvation from The Hellfire*. It is followed by the subsequent lines: *"Follow the Messenger in statement and actions — do not depart away from the Qurān. And take hold of the Ṣaḥiḥayn [i.e. the two authentic sources of revelation — the both of which are intermediaries for the connection of religion and faith. Read them with impartiality from whim, fanaticism, and partisan-spirit from Shayṭān. Make them both your judgment and do not judge against their contents in principle with the statement of any person."*

desires his soul's salvation" means from hellfire and from innovation.

His saying, "*listen to the statement of a sincere advisor and helper*" means one who is genuine in advising and helping you. So he is from the people of help and support.

2. Hold Fast to the Waḥiyy

كُنْ فِي أُمُورِكَ كُلِّهَا مُتَمَسِّكًا ... بِالوَحْيِ لاَ بِزَخَارِفِ الهَذَيَانِ

[2./(189.)] In all of your matters hold fast to the revelation and not to that of ornamented babble.

'Abd al-Rahmān al-Sa'dī (رحمه الله) explains:

Meaning: in both religious and temporal matters. So it is befitting that a student of knowledge holds fast to the two revelational sources. Everything besides the two revelational sources assumes their same ruling if they are derived from them or employed as a means [to understanding or implementing] them. Everything besides that is ornamented babbling. Either it will be harmful and of no benefit, or it will be benign, without harm or benefit. How could a person wanting salvation opt out of that which has verified benefit in favor of that which has no benefit? Knowledge is, as Shaykh al Islām stated, that which has evidence to support it, and that which is beneficial of it is that which came from the Messenger (صَلَّى اللهُ عَلَيْهِ وَسَلَّمَ). So the person seeks knowledge, firstly, to procure awareness of it, then he implements it, and then he invites others to it. It may be that his invitation is to done to guide an ignorant person, or to debate with an obstinate person so as to establish the proof against him. If he recants, then that is desired, however if he does not, then the person has excused himself and defended the religion.

Muhammad bin Sālih al 'Uthaymīn (رحمه الله) explains:

His saying, "*in all of your matters*" means in creed, moral character, worship, and interpersonal dealings.

In all of your matters, even in your clothing, eating, and drinking, be one who holds fast to the revelation that is inclusive of the Book and the Sunnah, and not to that of ornamented babble.

3. Support the Book & the Sunnah

وَانْصُر كِتَابَ اللهِ والسُّنَنَ الَّتِي ... جَاءَتْ عَنِ المَبْعُوثِ بِالفُرْقَانِ

[3./(190.)] Support Allah's Book and those Sunan that have come from the one who was dispatched with the Criterion.

'Abd al-Rahmān al-Sa'dī (رحمه الله) explains:

This is because aiding these two is sometimes done by the sword and weaponry, and sometimes it is done by proof and the tongue, which could be more impactful. This is just as has come in the ḥadīth:

أَفْضَلُ الْجِهَادِ: كَلِمَةُ حَقٍّ عِنْدَ سُلْطَانٍ جَائِرٍ

"The most meritorious jihād is a statement of truth to an oppressive *sulṭān* (lit., ruler/authority)."[10]

Muhammad bin Sālih al 'Uthaymīn (رَحِمَهُ ٱللَّهُ) explains:

His saying, "*support Allah's book*" means by defending it and by explaining its laws, innermost wisdoms, and meanings. That is what constitutes supporting the *Qurān*. Supporting it is not merely done by way of its recital, but rather, supporting it is by you defending it, and by explaining its laws, innermost wisdoms, and tremendous amazing subjects. Likewise is the case with "*the Sunan [i.e., prophetic traditions] that came from the one who was dispatched.*" This means that we must first make sure to verify that the specific Sunnah practice came from the Prophet (صَلَّى ٱللَّهُ عَلَيْهِ وَسَلَّمَ). Not everything ascribed to him is authentic, rather you must first research its chain of narration. If it is authentic, then you look at the reported text. Thenceforth you proceed to support what came from the Messenger (صَلَّى ٱللَّهُ عَلَيْهِ وَسَلَّمَ).

4. Strike the People of Falsehood with the Truth

وَاضْرِبْ بِسَيْفِ الوَحْيِ كُلَّ مُعَطِّلٍ ... ضَرْبَ المُجَاهِدِ فَوْقَ كُلِّ بَنَانِ

[4./(191.)] And strike down every mu'aṭṭil [i.e., negator] with the sword of the revelation — with the blow of a Mujāhid striking every joint.

---

[10] Collected by Aḥmad (18830) and al-Nasā'ī (4209)on the authority of Ṭāriq bin Shihāb (رَضِيَ ٱللَّهُ عَنْهُ). Graded Ṣaḥīḥ by al Albānī in Ṣaḥīḥ al Jāmi' al-Ṣaghīr (1100).

Aḥmad bin 'Īsā al-Najdī (رَحِمَهُ ٱللَّهُ) explains:

"*Strike with the sword of revelation*": The revelation comprises of beneficial knowledge and decisive evidence, not the ornamented assertions of the speculative theologians or the babbling of philosophers and mystics[II] which disconnect one away from Allah (عَزَّوَجَلَّ) and His Messenger (صَلَّىٱللَّهُعَلَيْهِوَسَلَّمَ). Anyone who follows that or gives it precedence to the clear revelation and unmistakable methodology — which is Allah's mighty book and the Sunnah of His truthful, trustworthy Messenger (صَلَّىٱللَّهُعَلَيْهِوَسَلَّمَ) — has deviated from the straight path. How commendable is the statement of the person who said:

العِلْمُ قَالَ اللهُ قَالَ رَسُولُهُ ... قَالَ الْصَّحَابَةُ لَيْسَ خُلْفٌ فِيهِ

Knowledge is what Allah said, what the Prophet (صَلَّىٱللَّهُعَلَيْهِوَسَلَّمَ) said, and what the Ṣaḥāba said — which is incontrovertible.

مَا الْعِلْمُ نَصْبُكَ لِلْخِلَافِ سَفَاهَةً ... بَيْنَ الْرَّسُولِ وَبَيْنَ رَأْيِ سَفِيهِ

Knowledge is not foolishly assigning contrarian differing between the Messenger (صَلَّىٱللَّهُعَلَيْهِوَسَلَّمَ) and a fools opinion.

[II] Ibn al Qayyim رَحِمَهُ ٱللَّهُ quoted at length a strong criticism of the *ḥanbalite faqīh* Ibn 'Aqīl رَحِمَهُ ٱللَّهُ against the speculative theologians and gnostic mystics:

> All of them are renegades against the matters of religion: this one audaciously speaks about issues that have explicit scriptural evidence — countering such evidence with what he claims to be the conclusion of reason; while the other says: my heart has spoken to me on behalf of my Lord... **There is nothing more harmful against the religion than the innovating theologians and the ignorant mystics:** the (former) corrupt the intellects with speculations and doubts that resemble what is rational; while (the latter) corrupt the deeds.

Ibn al Qayyim then comments:

> This is the speech of one (i.e. Ibn 'Aqīl) who once joined alongside the philosophers to the furthest extent and experienced the epitome of what they possess. He engaged in philosophical speculation and then shunned it, intimately knowing its scope and its furthest bounds. [Al-Ṣawā'iq vol. 4, p. 1342-1351].

كَلَّا وَلَا نَصْبُ الْخِلَافِ جَهَالَةً ... بَيْنَ النُّصُوصِ وَبَيْنَ رَأْيِ فَقِيهِ

Furthermore, it is not ignorantly assigning differing between the texts and the opinion of a jurist.

كَلَّا وَلَا رَدُّ النُّصُوصِ تَعَمُّدًا ... حَذرًا مِنَ التَّجْسِيمِ وَالتَّشْبِيهِ

Furthermore it is not intentionally rejecting the text out of [ostensible] caution from anthropomorphism.

حَاشَا النُّصُوصِ مِنَ الَّذِي رُمِيَتْ بِهِ ... مِنْ فِرْقَةِ التَّعْطِيلِ وَالتَّمْوِيهِ

The texts are innocent of what they are accused of by the sect of negators and distorters.

'Abd al-Raḥmān al-Sa'dī (رحمه الله) explains:

The word "*sword*" is used metaphorically in reference to the revelation. This is an allusion as to how it cuts off the disputant because the revelation is a clear-cut scriptural and rational proof.

Since the context is indicative of *ta'ṭīl* [i.e., negating divine attributes] he explicitly mentions that. Otherwise, everything that opposes the Book and the Sunnah is struck down with the sword of revelation.

That is because a person could be vulnerable due to a paucity of determination, so here he instructs a person pertaining that. Also, he could be vulnerable due to his paucity in knowledge, so he had instructed him previously to "*Be one who, in all of your affairs adheres to...*" He does the same later on: "*Make Allah's Book and the Sunan that are authentically established your weapon.*"

When these two are combined, then the intended goal is attained and perfection is achieved.

Muhammad bin Sālih al 'Uthaymīn (رَحِمَهُ ٱللَّهُ) explains:

He said, "***Strike with the sword of revelation.***" When you strike with the sword of revelation, will you be victorious or defeated? The answer is victorious. The evidence for this is Allah's statement (تَبَارَكَ وَتَعَالَىٰ):

﴿ بَلْ نَقْذِفُ بِالْحَقِّ عَلَى الْبَاطِلِ فَيَدْمَغُهُ فَإِذَا هُوَ زَاهِقٌ ﴾

"Rather, We dash the truth upon falsehood, and it destroys it, and thereupon it is departed." [al Anbiyā': 18]

Look at these tremendous words: (نقذف) means We [i.e., Allah (عَزَّوَجَلَّ) in His Greatness] will launch with rapidity.
(على الباطل فيدمغه) "*Against falsehood, and it destroys it*" means that it will strike it in the center of its brain. Will it then remain alive or will it die immediately? The answer is that it will die immediately. As such, the phrase (فإذا) denoting surprise is used. He said: (فإذا هو زاهق) "and suddenly it is departed" [i.e., in the noun form]. He did not say (يزهق) "and then it departs" [i.e., in the verb form].

So His saying (فإذا هو زاهق) denotes that it dies instantaneously. The one saying this is Allah — whose promise is the truth, whose statement is reality, and who is able to do this. So here he [i.e., Ibn al Qayyim (رَحِمَهُ ٱللَّهُ)] is commanding us to strike every denier with "*the sword of revelation*," and how tremendous of a sword it is! How effectively it eradicates and cuts through falsehood! However, if one were to say that we may find those who launch the truth against falsehood, yet this does not happen, then we respond that the defect is not with the weapon but rather it is with the weapon's brandisher.

Not everyone who brandishes a sword can inflict fatality with it. If the coward has a sword with him when the enemy approaches, then what will his stance be? The answer is that he will tremble and shake until he drops the sword! As for the brave one, then even if he had a stick, he would not fear the enemies' swords. So the reality is that the weapon is dependent on its brandisher.

Otherwise, the *Qurān* remains the *Qurān* and the *Sunnah* remains the *Sunnah*. The truth remains the truth and falsehood remains falsehood, but the defect is in the one carrying out the action.

5. Determination

وَاحْمِلْ بِعَزْمِ الصِّدْقِ حَمْلَةَ مُخْلِصٍ ... مُتَجَرِّدٍ لِلّهِ غَيْرِ جَبَانِ

[5./(192.)] And bear against them with genuine determination — with the advancing of someone sincere — exclusively for Allah, not being a coward.

'Abd al-Rahmān al-Sa'dī (رَحِمَهُ اللَّهُ) explains:

His statement "*with the advancing of someone sincere*" entails sincerity, whereas "*with exclusive devotion for Allah, not being a coward*" entails praiseworthy courage.

Muhammad bin Sālih al 'Uthaymīn (رَحِمَهُ ٱللَّهُ) explains:

He orders us to advance with genuine determination, with the advancing of someone sincere, exclusively for Allah (عَزَّوَجَلَّ), and not for the sake of personal desire or so that one's statement can be supreme. Rather, one is to be exclusively devoted to Allah (عَزَّوَجَلَّ). The person that advances for Allah's sake with a sincere intention and genuine determination will not be intimidated because the extent of the worst that could possibly happen is his being killed. However, if he is killed then that happens in Allah's path. He then moves on from the world of misery, unsettledness, and abuse to the world of bliss; so he does not care. This is similar to what Khālid bin al Walīd (رَضِيَ ٱللَّهُ عَنْهُ) wrote to Hurmuz, the Persian king:

"I have come to you with a people who love death as you love life."

This is a tremendous statement. It means that we love to die in Allah's path just as you love life, meaning that we do not care.

6. Firmness & Patience

وَاثْبُتْ بِصَبْرِكَ تَحْتَ أَلْوِيَةِ الهُدَى ... فَإِذَا أُصِبْتَ فَفِي رِضَا الرَّحْمَنِ

[6./(193.)] Be firm in your patience under the banner of guidance. So that when you are struck then that will be for Allah's Good-Pleasure.

'Abd al-Rahmān al-Sa'dī (رَحِمَهُ ٱللَّهُ) explains:

His statement, "*be firm in your patience under the banners of guidance*" is owing to the fact that victory comes through patience, just as occurs in the ḥadīth. Shaykh al Islām (رَحِمَهُ ٱللَّهُ) said:

بِالْعِلْمِ وَالْيَقِينِ تُنَالُ الْإِمَامَةُ فِي الدِّينِ

"By patience and certainty, leadership in achieved in the religion."

So whoever does not have patience will not achieve the objective, not even partially. His statement, "*so if you are stricken*" i.e., with death or anything less, "*then that will be within Allah's Good-Pleasure.*"

Muhammad bin Sālih al 'Uthaymīn (رَحِمَهُ ٱللَّهُ) explains:

He is saying: be firm, and if it is conceivable that you be struck, then that entails Allah's Good-Pleasure. Being stricken in a manner entailing Allah's Good-Pleasure is, in reality, not affliction, but rather it is the highest aim for which a person could wish. If he is stricken for Allah's sake, in a manner included within His Good-Pleasure, then he has not been stricken in reality, but rather he has attained reward and virtue. This last part "*so that when you are struck then that will be for Allah's Good-Pleasure*" is mandatory to be in the heart of every person.

Know that the person inviting to Allah (عَزَّوَجَلَّ) will inexorably encounter abuse, either verbally or physically, as Allah (تَبَارَكَ وَتَعَالَىٰ) said:

﴿ وَكَذَٰلِكَ جَعَلْنَا لِكُلِّ نَبِيٍّ عَدُوًّا مِّنَ الْمُجْرِمِينَ ۗ وَكَفَىٰ بِرَبِّكَ هَادِيًا وَنَصِيرًا ﴾

"And thus have We made for every prophet an enemy from among the criminals. But sufficient is your Lord as a guide and a helper." [al Furqān: 31].

So every prophet had enemies from the criminals and every person who inherits the Prophets' legacy (عَلَيْهِمُ السَّلَامُ) will have an enemy from the criminals. So abuse must happen as well as some harassment that you hear with your ears or are informed about. However, what should your stance be? Certainly, everything or the sort that befalls a person is for the sake of Allah's Good-Pleasure. As such, when the Prophet's finger was bloodied, what did he say? He (صَلَّىٰ ٱللَّهُ عَلَيْهِ وَسَلَّمَ) said:

هل أَنْتِ إِلَّا إِصْبَعٌ دَمِيتِ وَفِي سَبِيلِ اللهِ ما لَقِيتِ.

"Aren't you just a finger that bled, and wasn't what you encountered in Allah's Path?"[12]

So long as a person endures abuse for undertaking Allah's commandments, then let him rejoice at goodness. For indeed this is from the meritorious stations of the Prophets (عَلَيْهِمُ السَّلَامُ). Do not be like those about whom Allah said:

[12] Collected by al Bukhārī (2648), and Muslim (1796).

﴿وَمِنَ النَّاسِ مَن يَقُولُ آمَنَّا بِاللَّهِ فَإِذَا أُوذِيَ فِي اللَّهِ جَعَلَ فِتْنَةَ النَّاسِ كَعَذَابِ اللَّهِ﴾

"And of the people are some who say, "We believe in Allah," but when one [of them] is harmed for [the cause of] Allah, they consider the trial of the people as [if it were] the punishment of Allah." [al 'Ankabūt: 10].

Then they apostatized. Rather, you are to be firm!

II. Brandishing the Weapon of Truth
Synopsis of Lines 7-13:

7. Brandishing the Sword of Truth

8. Having Audacity against Falsehood

9. & 10. Proclaim the Truth,
Even with Few Supporters;
Allah Aids the Religion

11. The Reality of their Plots

12. Angels vs. Devils

13. Contrast the Two Sides

II. Brandishing the Weapon of Truth

وَاجْعَلْ كِتَابَ اللهِ وَالسُّنَنَ الَّتِي ... ثَبَتَتْ سِلَاحَكَ ثُمَّ صِحِ بِجَنَانِ

[7./(194.)] Make as your weapon Allah's Book and those Sunan that are authentically established, and then scream with all of your heart:

مَنْ ذَا يُبَارِزْ فَلْيُقَدِّمْ نَفْسَهُ ... أَوْ مَنْ يُسَابِقْ يَبْدُ فِي المَيْدَانِ

[8./(195.)] Who wants to contend? Then let him bring himself forward! Who wants to race forward? Then let him step onto the field!

وَاصْدَعْ بِمَا قَالَ الرَّسُولُ وَلَا تَخَفْ ... مِنْ قِلَّةِ الأَنْصَارِ وَالأَعْوَانِ

[9./(196.)] Boldly proclaim what the Messenger said and do not be fearful of having few supporters and helpers.

فَاللهُ نَاصِرُ دِينِهِ وَكِتَابِهِ ... وَاللهُ كَافٍ عَبْدَهُ بِأَمَانِ

[10./(197.)] Allah is the Aider of His religion and His Book. And Allah is the Sufficer for His worshipper by way of protection.

لَا تَخْشَ مِنْ كَيْدِ العَدُوِّ وَمَكْرِهِمْ ... فَقِتَالُهُمْ بِالْكِذْبِ وَالبُهْتَانِ

[11./(198.)] Do not fear the plot of the enemy and their conspiring. For indeed they fight by means of lying and slander.

فَجُنُودُ أَتْبَاعِ الرَّسُولِ مَلَائِكٌ ... وَجُنُودُهُمْ فَعَسَاكِرُ الشَّيْطَانِ

[12./(199.)] The armies of the Messenger's followers are angels, whereas their armies [i.e., the people of falsehood] are the troops of Satan.

شَتَّانَ بَيْنَ العَسْكَرَيْنِ فَمَنْ يَكُنْ ... مُتَحَيِّراً فَلْيَنْظُرِ الفِئَتَانِ

[13. /(200.)] How great is the difference between the two armies! So whoever wants to pick a side then let him contrast the two parties.

Synopsis of Lines 7-13

Muhammad Khalīl Harrās (رَحِمَهُ ٱللَّهُ) summarizes:

Similarly, he [i.e., Ibn al Qayyim (رَحِمَهُ ٱللَّهُ)] advises him to make Allah's Book and the authentic, verified reports of Sunnah as his weapon and apparatus during the conflict. So once he is wearing this armor and completes due preparations, then he is to scream out: is there anyone to duel or contend? For indeed, he has the most powerful and effectual weapon, and, as such, he does not fear the weapons of the people of falsehood which are ineffectual and blunt. He is to boldly proclaim what the Messenger (صَلَّى ٱللَّهُ عَلَيْهِ وَسَلَّمَ) said without feeling isolation on account of few supporters and the scarcity of helpers. For indeed, Allah (عَزَّ وَجَلَّ) is the Aider of His religion and Book. He is enough and is sufficient for him. He is not to fear the harm and plots of the enemy because they fight with the weapons of lying and slander, whereas he fights with the weapon of monotheism and faith. How tremendous of a difference is there between the two weapons! This is similar to how he fights them with an army of angels, whereas they have the legions of Satan as their army. So how great a divergence there is between the two armies and how clear a distinction there is between the two factions!

﴿ قَدْ كَانَ لَكُمْ آيَةٌ فِي فِئَتَيْنِ الْتَقَتَا ۖ فِئَةٌ تُقَاتِلُ فِي سَبِيلِ اللَّهِ وَأُخْرَىٰ كَافِرَةٌ يَرَوْنَهُم مِّثْلَيْهِمْ رَأْيَ الْعَيْنِ ۚ وَاللَّهُ يُؤَيِّدُ بِنَصْرِهِ مَن يَشَاءُ ۗ إِنَّ فِي ذَٰلِكَ لَعِبْرَةً لِّأُولِي الْأَبْصَارِ ﴾

"Already there has been for you a sign in the two armies which met - one fighting in the cause of Allah and another of disbelievers. They saw them [to be] twice their [own] number by [their] eyesight. But Allah supports with His victory whom He wills. Indeed in that is a lesson for those of vision."[Aal 'Imrān: 13]

7. Brandishing the Sword of Truth

وَاجْعَلْ كِتَابَ اللهِ وَالسُّنَنَ الَّتِي ... ثَبَتَتْ سِلَاحَكَ ثُمَّ صِحْ بِجَنَانِ

[7./(194.)] Make as your weapon Allah's Book and those Sunan that are authentically established, and then scream with all of your heart:

'Abd al-Raḥmān al-Sa'dī (رحمه الله) explains:

As for his statement: "*Make Allah's book,*" then since the book [i.e., the *Qurān*] is authentically established he did not mention any modifier, while on the other hand there are some ḥadīth that are authentic while others are inauthentic and, as such, are not utilized for evidence. Thus, he modified it with a conditional phrase by saying: "*the Sunan* ***that are authentically established.***"

"*(Make these) your weapon and then scream with all of your heart.*" (Meaning) while maintaining focus and composure, say with your heart: "*Who wants to contend? Then let him bring himself forward! Who wants to challenge? Then let him step onto the field!*"

Muhammad bin Sālih al 'Uthaymīn (رحمه الله) explains:

He said, "*[scream] with your heart*" and in another version [he said] "*bi-jabān*" [i.e., at the coward]. I think that "*at the coward*" is clearer, meaning scream at the cowards and say: "*who wants to contend.*" This is because "*scream with the janān*" means scream with the heart, requiring further elaboration. It would mean: scream with your tongue with a scream that exits from your heart. Whatever the case, then if the version is like this — according to the author's compilation of this poem — then the meaning of "*scream with your heart*" is scream out a scream that emanates from your *janān*, meaning your heart. If it was "*at the cowards,*" then that is even clearer because when a person yells at cowards, then they disperse at his mere scream. As such, it is mentioned that some of the courageous, upon flanking the enemy and simply yelling, would cause the cavalry to disperse. The cavalry would be disbanded by his mere scream to such an extent that some of the horsemen would say that the horse's spirit would collapse at the scream of this sort of brave man.

The meaning is: make the Qurān and Sunnah the weapon. His saying "*then scream out*" means yell out at the cowardly (foe) by quoting these two sources. What will be the cowards condition at that point? Will he stand firm or flee? The answer is that he will flee. He cannot possibly remain in place so long as your weapon is the Book and the Sunnah and so long as you have the strength — strength of determination and strength of initiation. At that point, then know that nothing can remain in front of you.

Thus, he is saying make your weapon consist of two things: Allah's Book and the *Sunan* that are authentically established. This is not said about everything that is called *Sunnah*, rather, in order for them to be used as your weaponry, the matters of *Sunnah* must be authentically established Then scream at these cowards saying: *who wants to contend?* Is anyone able to truly contend against someone whose weapon is Allah's Book and the Sunnah of His Messenger (ﷺ) while this contender has nothing as a weapon but babble, lying, fabrication, guile, and ornamented speech? Will he be able to do so or not? The answer is that he will never be able to do so. A single verse from Allah's book demolishes all that he produces of ornamented speech until it is obliterated.

8. Having Audacity against Falsehood

ذَا يُبَارِزْ فَلْيُقَدِّمْ نَفْسَهُ ... أَوْ مَنْ يُسَابِقْ يَبْدُ فِي المَيْدَانِ

[8./(195.)] Who wants to contend? Then let him bring himself forward! Who wants to race forward? Then let him step onto the field!

Muhammad bin Sālih al 'Uthaymīn (رحمه الله) explains:

His saying, "*who wants to contend*" means yell out to the cowards saying: "*whoever wants to contend, then let him come forward and whoever wants to race forward, then let him step onto the field.*"

The meaning of *al mubāraza* is exiting. It derives from the verb *baraza, yabruzu* — when someone exits. From their [i.e., the early Arabs] customs was that when two armies would meet, they would challenge the enemy's brave-hearted to contend with them. The benefit of contenting was that once the contender was defeated it would serve as attrition of their power and strike them with fear and dread. This is something well-known from the ways of soldiers.

9. & 10. Proclaim the Truth, Even with Few Supporters; Allah Aids the Religion

وَاصْدَعْ بِمَا قَالَ الرَّسُولُ وَلَا تَخَفْ ... مِنْ قِلَّةِ الأَنْصَارِ وَالأَعْوَانِ

[9./(196.)] Boldly proclaim what the Messenger said and do not be fearful from having few supporters and helpers.

فَاللّٰهُ نَاصِرُ دِينِهِ وَكِتَابِهِ ... وَاللّٰهُ كَافٍ عَبْدَهُ بِأَمَانِ

[10./(197.)] Allah is the Aider of His religion and His Book. And Allah is the Sufficer for His worshipper by way of protection.

Muhammad bin Sālih al 'Uthaymīn (رَحِمَهُ ٱللَّهُ) explains:

We have been commanded to boldly proclaim what the Messenger (صَلَّى ٱللَّهُ عَلَيْهِ وَسَلَّمَ) said, not being afraid of having few supporters and helpers. Even if you are by yourself, then yes, you are to proclaim what the Prophet (صَلَّى ٱللَّهُ عَلَيْهِ وَسَلَّمَ) said and not be afraid of having few supporters. Even more-so, do not fear the many who stand against you and oppose you. The one who boldly proclaims what the Messenger (صَلَّى ٱللَّهُ عَلَيْهِ وَسَلَّمَ) said will either: (1.) find support, or (2.) he will not find any support, or (3.) he will find opposition. As for the first person — the one who finds support — then it is clear that he will boldly proclaim (the truth), because he is accompanied by those who will aid him. As for the second —the one who does not experience this or that (i.e., support or opposition) but rather encounters apathy — this person may also become lazy when he finds that no-one shows interest in the Messenger's statements that he proclaims. As for the third: the one who is encountered and confronted with opposition that attempts to permanently stop him by way of constriction and propaganda — then none of this should amount to anything in front of the person.

This does not apply exclusively to matters of creed, but it pertains to creed, *fiqh* rulings, manners, and character. In every regard, you must proclaim what the Messenger (صَلَّى ٱللَّهُ عَلَيْهِ وَسَلَّمَ) said in both word and deed and not care about any of this. Even if all you have in front of you are those who are apathetic or those who are in opposition, then that cannot worry you.

"*Allah is the Aider of His religion and His Book. And Allah is the Sufficer for His worshipper by way of protection.*"

What he said is true. Allah (عَزَّوَجَلَّ) is the Aider of His religion and He is His worshipper's Sufficer by way of protection. However, when will he suffice him? The answer is when he trusts in Him. Allah (تَبَارَكَ وَتَعَالَىٰ) said:

﴿وَمَن يَتَوَكَّلْ عَلَى اللَّهِ فَهُوَ حَسْبُهُ﴾

"And whoever relies upon Allah - then He is sufficient for him." [al-Ṭalāq: 3]

11. The Reality of their Plots

لاَ تَخْشَ مِنْ كَيْدِ العَدْوِّ وَمَكْرِهِمْ ... فَقِتَالُهُمْ بِالْكِذْبِ وَالبُهْتَانِ

[11./(198.)] Do not fear enemy's plotting and conspiring. For indeed they fight by means of lying and slander.

Sālih al Fawzān (حفظه الله) explains:

Meaning: Once you have armed yourself with the Book, the Sunnah, and beneficial knowledge, then at that point you can seek to contend with the opposers. As for prior to arming yourself, then do not enter into debating. The person must learn before entering into the arena of discussion, refutation, and disputation. So after you have armed yourself with the Book and the *Sunnah*, you will never be defeated, whereas if you do not have knowledge, then you will be swept away by the first doubt that is presented. If you have a weapon consisting of the Book and the *Sunnah*, then all that they possess is lying and slandering. Lying and slandering cannot subsist against the Book and the Sunnah.

Muhammad bin Sālih al 'Uthaymīn (رحمه الله) explains:

He is saying: do not fear the plots and machinations of these people, because they fight by lying and slandering, and by way of false, misleading, ornamented speech. However, this — meaning not fearing their plots and conspiring — requires strong ambition and genuine determination.

12. Angels vs. Devils

فَجُنُودُ أَتْبَاعِ الرَّسُولِ مَلَائِكٌ ... وَجُنُودُهُمْ فَعَسَاكِرُ الشَّيْطَانِ

[12./(199.)] The armies of the Messenger's followers are angels, whereas their armies [i.e., the people of falsehood] are the troops of Satan.

'Abd al-Rahmān al-Sa'dī (رَحِمَهُ ٱللَّهُ) explains:

His statement: "*The armies of the Messenger's followers are angels,*" means that their internal army consists of holding fast to the revelation while having sincerity and patience. Their external army are the angels of al-Raḥmān. As for those besides them, "*their armies are the troops of Satan.*" Their internal army comprises of lying and slandering, whereas their external army are the troops of Satan. As such, the author says: "*How great is the difference between the two armies! So whoever wants to pick a side then let him look at both parties.*"

Sālih al Fawzān (حفظه الله) explains:

The angels of al-Raḥmān, (such as) Jibrīl, Mikā'īl, and the other angels are your helpers. On the other hand, their [i.e., the people of falsehood's] helpers are the army of Satan. The devils undoubtedly cannot stand against the angels. Indeed during the battle of Badr, when Satan saw the angels, he fled. (Allah) (تَبَارَكَ وَتَعَالَىٰ) said:

﴿ فَلَمَّا تَرَاءَتِ الْفِئَتَانِ نَكَصَ عَلَىٰ عَقِبَيْهِ وَقَالَ إِنِّي بَرِيءٌ مِّنكُمْ إِنِّي أَرَىٰ مَا لَا تَرَوْنَ إِنِّي أَخَافُ اللَّهَ ۚ وَاللَّهُ شَدِيدُ الْعِقَابِ ﴾

"But when the two armies sighted each other, he [i.e., Iblīs] turned on his heels and said, 'Indeed, I am disassociated from you. Indeed, I see what you do not see; indeed I fear Allah. And Allah is severe in penalty.'" [al Anfāl: 48].

The followers of truth have angels with them, whereas the followers of falsehood in every era have devils with them. The devils could never stand against the angels.

Muhammad bin Sālih al 'Uthaymīn (رَحِمَهُ ٱللَّٰهُ) explains:

He is saying that the army of these people are the troops of Satan, whereas the armies of the Messenger (صَلَّى ٱللَّٰهُ عَلَيْهِ وَسَلَّمَ) are the angels of al-Raḥmān, just as Allah (تَبَارَكَ وَتَعَالَىٰ) said:

﴿ إِذْ يُوحِي رَبُّكَ إِلَى الْمَلَائِكَةِ أَنِّي مَعَكُمْ فَثَبِّتُوا الَّذِينَ آمَنُوا ﴾

"[Remember] when your Lord inspired to the angels, 'I am with you, so strengthen those who have believed.'" [al Anfāl: 12].

So the angels reinforce and support Allah's worshippers. As such, the Messenger (صَلَّى ٱللَّٰهُ عَلَيْهِ وَسَلَّمَ) used to say to Ḥassān bin Thābit (رَضِيَ ٱللَّٰهُ عَنْهُ) while he recited poetry (to lampoon the enemy on the battlefield):

اللَّهُمَّ أَيِّدْهُ بِرُوحِ الْقُدُس

"Oh Allah! Support him with al-Ruḥ al Qudus [i.e., Jibrīl]"[13]

For this reason, when a person is engaged in the *jihād* of knowledge and clarifying, he feels inspiration that he does not experience during a state of ease. That is because of the angels reinforcing him and due to the doors of knowledge being opened for him.

13. Contrast the Two Sides

شَتَّانَ بَيْنَ العَسْكَرَيْنِ فَمَنْ يَكُنْ ... مُتَحَيِّراً فَلْيَنْظُرِ الفِئَتَانِ

[13. /(200.)] How great is the difference between the two armies! So whoever is bewildered then let him contrast the two parties.

Muhammad bin Sālih al 'Uthaymīn (رحمه الله) explains:

It has come worded as "*mutaḥayyir,*" [bewildered] meaning: he who doubts as to which of the two are upon the truth. Another version says "*mutahayyiz*" [i.e., one who chooses a side in a dispute or skirmish]. The first is most appropriate. Meaning that it is mandatory that a person knows the difference between this and that. Whoever is bewildered, then let him look and reflect until he recognizes those who are most rightful to be followed.

[13] Collected by Bukhārī (3040), and Muslim (2485).

III. How to Overcome The People of Falsehood Synopsis of Lines 14-20:

14. Victory comes with Patience

15. Remember the Past

16. Use the Texts Against Them

17. Do Not Be Intimidated by Their Numbers

18. Preoccupy Them with Each Other

19. Do Not Fear Their Advance

20. Wait for Adequate Support

III. How to Overcome the People of Falsehood

وَاثْبُتْ وَقَاتِلْ تَحْتَ رَايَاتِ الهُدَى ... وَاصْبِرْ فَنَصْرُ اللهِ رَبِّكَ دَانِ

[14. /(201.)] Be firm and fight under the banners of guidance. And be patient, for indeed the help of Allah, your Lord, is near.

وَاذْكُرْ مَقَاتِلَهُمْ لِفُرْسَانِ الهُدَى ... لِلَّهِ دَرُّ مَقَاتِلِ الفُرْسَانِ

[15. /(202.)] Mention their fatal flaws to the cavalry of guidance, How commendable is it to tell the cavalry where to strike!

وَادْرَأْ بِلَفْظِ النَّصِّ فِي نَحْرِ العِدَا ... وَارْجُمْهُمْ بِثَوَاقِبِ الشُّهْبَانِ

[16. /(203.)] Push back with the wordings of the texts against the enemy front, and launch rapid balls of fire at them.

لاَ تَخْشَ كَثْرَتَهُمْ فَهُمْ هَمَجُ الوَرَى ... وَذُبَابُهُ أَتَخَافُ مِنْ ذِبَّانِ

[17. /(204.)] Do not fear their numbers, for they are the rabble and flies of creation. Or are you afraid of flies?

وَاشْغَلْهُمْ عِنْدَ الجِدَالِ بِبَعْضِهِمْ ... بَعْضاً فَذَاكَ الحَزْمُ لِلْفُرْسَانِ

[18. /(205.)] When debating them, preoccupy them with each other. That affords ḥazm (resoluteness) to the horsemen.

وَإِذَا هُمْ حَمَلُوا عَلَيْكَ فَلَا تَكُنْ ... فَزِعاً لِحَمْلَتِهِمْ وَلَا بِجَبَانِ

[19. /(206.)] And when they bear down upon you then do not be frightened at their offense and do not be a coward.

وَاثْبُتْ وَلَا تَحْمِلْ بِلاَ جُنْدٍ فَمَا ... هَذَا بِمَحْمُودٍ لَدَى الشُّجْعَانِ

[20. /(207.)] Be firm and do not launch an offense without an army for that is not commendable with those who are brave.

Synopsis of Lines 14-20

Muhammad Khalīl Harrās (رحمه الله) summarizes:

The author repeats the advice to the seeker of salvation, namely, that he is to remain resolute beneath the banner of guidance, holding fast to Allah's rope while maintaining patience, being hopeful of reward, and having certainty that Allah's help is near. He is to point the calvary of guidance and army of truth towards the fatal flaws of these foes, namely, the points of attack that eventuate in their end. He is to push against their frontlines with the verified wordings of the texts, launching blazing meteors against them.

He is not to fear their numerical abundance or the extremity of their clamoring and noise making, for certainly they are rabble-rousing gnats that prove irresolute at the moment of contact. Rather, they are even less significant than these flies who, despite their loud buzzing, are incapable of doing anything.

Although these foes are a single mob against the people of truth, then they are simultaneously in conflict between themselves. Resoluteness dictates that we distract them from skirmishing with us by preoccupying them with each other. That benefits us because it familiarizes us with the harm of

combatting them collectively, and beyond that, they ultimately injure each other.
However, when they make peace between each other in order to conduct war and go on the offense against us, then it is mandatory that we do are not disheartened by their attack, nor are we to be cowardly while confronting them during the conflict. We are to amass our forces to contend with them, for indeed, engaging without soldiers and supporters is not commendable in the estimation of the heroic and brave.

14. Victory comes with Patience

وَاثْبُتْ وَقَاتِلْ تَحْتَ رَايَاتِ الهُدَى ... وَاصْبِرْ فَنَصْرُ اللهِ رَبِّكَ دَانِ

[14. /(201.)] Be firm and fight under the banners of guidance (i.e., defend the truth and repudiate falsehood). And be patient, for indeed the help of Allah, your Lord, is near

Muhammad bin Sālih al 'Uthaymīn (رحمه الله) explains:

This is similar to the first instance [i.e., line 6/(183)], but he repeated it here for additional reinforcement of the person's heart.

15. Remember the Past

وَاذْكُرْ مَقَاتِلَهُمْ لِفُرْسَانِ الهُدَى ... لِلَّهِ دَرُّ مَقَاتِلِ الفُرْسَانِ

[15. /(202.)] Mention their fatal flaws to the horsemen of guidance, How commendable is it to tell the horsemen where to strike!

'Abd al-Raḥmān al-Sa'dī (رحمه الله) explains:

His statement: "*Mention their maqātil*" meaning the occasions of their defeat and the events that transpired in the past between them and the cavalry of guidance. Meaning: mention *Ahl al-Sunnah's* debates with them during which they educated them and vanquished their arguments, such as: the debate of al-Shaykh 'Abd al 'Azīz al Kanānī with Bishr al Marīsī, and Imām Aḥmad's debate with the *Jahmites*. This aids in explaining their falsehood and clarifying the truth.

Sālih al Fawzān (حفظه الله) explains:

Recall what happened during the battles of Badr, Ḥunayn, and other occasions where Allah (عَزَّوَجَلَّ) gave the Muslims victory. Remember what happened during the battle against the Mongols and how the Muslims fought them. {Likewise is the case with} how the Crusaders were vanquished at the hand of Ṣalāḥ ul-Dīn.

Muhammad bin Sālih al 'Uthaymīn (رحمه الله) explains:

Its meaning is: expose their flaws. So it befitting amongst ourselves that we clarify their fatal flaws, meaning: their places of fatality in order to fatally wound them **through that which disproves their statements.**

So we say use this or that to debate or dispute with them, just as al-Shāfi'ī said about the *Qadariyyah*:

نَاظِرُوا الْقَدَرِيَّةَ بِالْعِلْمِ ، فَإِنْ أَقَرُّوا بِهِ خُصِمُوا وَإِنْ أَنْكَرُوا كَفَرُوا

"Debate the Qadariyyah (by mention of) Divine Knowledge. If they admit its affirmation, then they have lost the debate, and if they deny it, then they have disbelieved."

This is what is most appropriate: that you begin by mentioning their flaws. This is because if you began by mentioning the defect and people understood the flaw, then the vulnerability is exposed, and that person is then overwhelmed and immobilized.

16. Use the Texts Against Them

وَادْرَأْ بِلَفْظِ النَّصِّ فِي نَحْرِ العِدَا ... وَارْجُمْهُمْ بِثَوَاقِبِ الشُّهْبَانِ

[16. /(203.)] Repel the adversary with the wording of the texts, and launch rapid balls of fire at them.

'Abd al-Rahmān al-Sa'dī (رحمه الله) explains:

He said: "*repel the adversary with the wording of the texts*," because once you present them with the texts, then if they reject them, they commit unbelief. For indeed, when al Jahm rejected Allah's speaking and His *khullah* [i.e., special love], then they judged him to have disbelieved, after which he was executed.

On the other hand, if they concede to them (i.e., the wordings of the texts), which is what normally happens, only to then alter and misinterpret them, then at that point, their arrogance, pseudo-intellectualism, and stubbornness will become obvious to you and others.

Muhammad bin Sālih al 'Uthaymīn (رحمه الله) explains:

He said: (ادرأْ) meaning: repel.

He said: (فـي نحـر الـعدى) (lit. in the enemies neck) meaning in front of them. The meaning is: clarify the text. Do not make a departure to the right or the left, and do not distort. Mention the wording of the text, at which point they will be immobilized.

17. Do Not Be Intimidated by Their Numbers

لاَ تَخْشَ كَثْرَتَهُمْ فَهُمْ هَمَجُ الوَرَى ... وَذُبَابُهُ أَتَخَافُ مِنْ ذِبَّانِ

[17./(204.)] Do not fear their numbers, for they are the rabble and flies of creation. Or are you afraid of flies?

Ahmad bin 'Isā al-Najdī (رحمه الله) explains:

Hamaj are small mosquito-like flies that land on the faces and eyes of sheep and donkeys. It is said about imbecilic rabble that they are just *hamaj*. [*Mukhtār al-Ṣiḥāḥ*] The plural of a fly [*dhubāb*] is *adhibba* for a few and *ḍhibbān* for many, just as is the case with the plural forms for crow [*ghurāb*], which are *aghriba* and *ghirbān*. [*Mukhtār al-Ṣiḥāḥ*]

'Abd al-Rahmān al-Sa'dī (رحمه الله) explains:

He said: "Do not fear their numbers, for the are the *hamaj* of the faces and eyes of sheep and donkeys. In reference to idiotic rabble-rousers, it is said that they are *hamaj* [i.e., gnats].

Sālih al Fawzān (حفظه الله) *explains:*

Meaning: You are having an encounter with flies. Flies do not intimidate anyone. What is meant by fighting here is inclusive of fighting with the sword[14] as well as with evidence and clarification. This is because repelling the people of falsehood with evidence is comparable to repelling them with force of arms. (Allah) (تَبَارَكَ وَتَعَالَى) said:

﴿ يَا أَيُّهَا النَّبِيُّ جَاهِدِ الْكُفَّارَ وَالْمُنَافِقِينَ وَاغْلُظْ عَلَيْهِمْ ﴾

"O Prophet, struggle against the disbelievers and the hypocrites and be harsh upon them." [al-Tawbah: 73].

Struggle against the unbelievers by force of arms, and struggle against the hypocrites with evidence.

Muhammad bin Sālih al 'Uthaymīn (رحمه الله) *explains:*

The answer is that I am not afraid of swarming flies, or of gnats and rabble-rousers, even if they be many. For the truth is victorious, even if its followers are few, and falsehood is forsaken, even if its followers are many. So here he is saying that flies are from the most insignificant and frightened of

14 Ability, meaning adequate personnel and materiel strength, and lawful authority are some of the most important prerequisites of this type. As has been alluded to previously, this type is exclusively the domain of those charged with such authority in Muslim lands.

things. If you motioned like this with your hand — without even hitting it — it just flies away and does not come back towards you. So these people are the flies of humanity.

So the author used this similitude to clarify and expose the hideousness of their condition, because comparing a person to a fly is an undoubted ascription of hideousness, while it simultaneously explains their condition, being that it is from the weakest of insects.

18. Preoccupy Them with Each Other

وَاشْغَلْهُمْ عِنْدَ الجِدَالِ بِبَعْضِهِمِ ... بَعْضاً فَذَاكَ الحَزْمُ لِلْفُرْسَانِ

[18. /(205.)] When debating them, preoccupy them with each other. That affords resoluteness to the horsemen.

'Abd al-Raḥmān al-Sa'dī (رحمه الله) explains:

This causes disputation, splitting, and dispiritedness between them, causing them to then scheme against each other, thus sparing you from them in turn. Doing this also makes it easier to debate them, just as it also demonstrates the inauthenticity of their doctrines and aids the creed of the Salaf. You say to the *Khawārij* for example: What is your response to the *Rāfiḍah* on this issue? Or vice-versa. You say to the *Qadariyyah*: What is your response to the doctrine of the *Jabriyyah*? Or vice-versa. To the *Jabriyyah* you say: What do you say about the doctrine of the *Khawārij*? And vice-versa.

The author [i.e., Ibn al Qayyim (رحمه الله)] and his shaykh [i.e., Ibn Taymiyyah (رحمه الله)] mentioned many debates that happened between the innovators' conflicting, contradictory doctrines. Afterwords they proceed to mention the creed of the Salaf, at which point the sun would shine clearly for anyone with two eyes to see.

Sālih al Fawzān (حفظه الله) explains:

You will find them disunited, so preoccupy them with each other until they forget you and are weakened on account of that. This is because they are disunited. And all praise is for Allah.

﴿ تَحْسَبُهُمْ جَمِيعًا وَقُلُوبُهُمْ شَتَّىٰ ۚ ذَٰلِكَ بِأَنَّهُمْ قَوْمٌ لَّا يَعْقِلُونَ ﴾

"You think they are together, but their hearts are divided. That is because they are a people who do not reason." [al Ḥashr: 13].

This is contrary to the condition of the people of truth, they are united in their hearts and their bodies.

Muhammad bin Sālih al 'Uthaymīn (رحمه الله) explains:

This is also from the useful methods of debate. The people of innovation are contradictory in nature, thus they are not upon a single way. One of them will go so far as to say that something is mandated by logic while another says that it is logically impossible. So he says it is impossible, not even ceding to its possibility.

So he [i.e., Ibn al Qayyim (رحمه الله)] is saying: busy them with each other. If they are in front of you, then say: So-and-so, you purport such and such, and so-and-so, you say something else. Explain to me. If they are not in front of you, then expound upon what they say. Say that if someone says this-and-that to you, then someone else said this-and-that in response, yet what is correct is...(then mention the truth on that topic) and it is proven by the Book and the Sunnah. What is important is to strike them against each other, at which point they will suffice you from each other. This is a strategy that is even used in contemporary military matters. This is the practice of *Ahl al-Sunnah* with the people of speculative theology. As such, you find that Shaykh al Islām sometimes conveys the falsehood of their doctrines by showing that they are contradictory. He then says that so-and-so, one of their figureheads, says such-and-such, while so-and-so, another one of their figureheads, says such-and-such. This proves that there is contradiction. The contradictory nature of a doctrine is the greatest evidence of its falsity. Also, "divide and conquer" is a popular principle.

19. Do Not Fear Their Advance

وَإِذَا هُمْ حَمَلُوا عَلَيْكَ فَلَا تَكُنْ ... فَزِعاً لِحَمْلَتِهِمْ وَلَا بِجَبَانِ

[19. /(206.)] And when they bear down upon you then do not be frightened at their offense and do not be a coward.

'Abd al-Raḥmān al-Sa'dī (رحمه الله) explains:

Having fearfulness and cowardice are some of the worst flaws against you. Even if the truth was on your side while your opponent was upon falsehood, then you would be unable to bring forth your proof and support your statement if you were

Sālih al Fawzān (حفظه الله) explains:

This is because their onslaught — even if it appears to be powerful — will soon vanish, owing to the fact that it is built on falsehood and falsehood dissipates.

Muhammad bin Sālih al 'Uthaymīn (رحمه الله) explains:

When they all collectively advance against you, then do not fear, but rather be firm. Otherwise, they are all going to be against you. Look currently at the Jews and the Christians. They are enemies of each other, as Allah (تبارك وتعالى) said:

﴿ وَقَالَتِ الْيَهُودُ لَيْسَتِ النَّصَارَىٰ عَلَىٰ شَيْءٍ وَقَالَتِ النَّصَارَىٰ لَيْسَتِ الْيَهُودُ عَلَىٰ شَيْءٍ وَهُمْ يَتْلُونَ الْكِتَابَ ﴾

"The Jews say 'The Christians have nothing [true] to stand on,' and the Christians say, 'The Jews have nothing to stand on,' although they [both] recite the Scripture." [al Baqarah: 113].

Each renders judgement on the other as being astray, yet despite that, they are allies against the Muslims. Allah (تبارك وتعالى) said:

﴿ يَا أَيُّهَا الَّذِينَ آمَنُوا لَا تَتَّخِذُوا الْيَهُودَ وَالنَّصَارَىٰ أَوْلِيَاءَ ۘ بَعْضُهُمْ أَوْلِيَاءُ بَعْضٍ ﴾

"O you who have believed, do not take the Jews and the Christians as allies. They are [in fact] allies of one another." [al Mā'idah: 51].

This is despite them being enemies of each other, however they are all the same when they are against a mutual enemy.

20. Wait for Adequate Support

وَاثْبُتْ وَلَا تَحْمِلْ بِلَا جُنْدٍ فَمَا ... هَذَا بِمَحْمُودٍ لَدَى الشُّجْعَانِ

[20. /(207.)] Be firm and do not launch an offense without an army for that is not commendable with those who are brave.

'Abd al-Raḥmān al-Sa'dī (رحمه الله) explains:

As for his statement: "*So be firm and do not launch an offensive without an army*," then the person cannot approach debating until he possesses two matters:

The first is that he is knowledgeable of his creed as well as that of his opponent.

The second is that he is safe from physical attack.

These two matters constitute the aforementioned army. If a person is missing one or the other, then he cannot engage. In such an instance, the harms of doing so might be greater than the advantage, even if one's intention and desire was correct and good.

Sālih al Fawzān (حفظه الله) explains:

Do not enter onto the field unless you have a weapon to fight with, namely, the Book and the Sunnah; and unless you have helpers from the people of truth and Allah's army. Do not enter onto the field alone.

Muhammad bin Sālih al 'Uthaymīn (رحمه الله) explains:

His saying, "*be firm*" means in front of them. His saying, "*do not advance without an army*" means do not proceed forward unless you have an army with you, because it is not from wisdom that a person advances without an army. Likewise, do not advance without a weapon, for it is not from wisdom to advance without a weapon. Also, your weapon has to be compatible with the enemy's weaponry, otherwise you will be defeated. As such, some people rush to advance in combat the enemy without a weapon. Additionally, he may not have faith like the *Ṣaḥāba* did, so calamity and defeat results from that. What is important is that you do not advance without a weapon, nor do you advance without an army. As such, he said, "*for that is not commendable with those who are brave*."

As for his statement, "*without an army,*" then the author possibly intends "*an army*" in this instance to mean ***the scholars who aid and help you.*** It bears another possibility which is that he intends thereby having a weapon — ***meaning do not advance without knowledge***. However, the latter part of the author's speech supports the first possible meaning. For this reason he says thereafter, "*So when you see the faction of Islam* *have assembled with their regiments... then at that point, penetrate the ranks."*

IV. Necessary Qualities for Victory
Synopsis of Lines 21-27:

21. Strength in Unity

22. Do Not be Helpless, Complain or Be Fearful

23. Ridding Oneself of Loathsome Traits

24. Compound Ignorance & Blind Fanaticism

25. Objectivity & Fairness

26. Fearing Allah & Genuineness for the Messenger

27. Hold Fast & Place Your Trust in Allah

IV. Necessary Qualities for Victory

فَإِذَا رَأَيْتَ عِصَابَةَ الإِسْلَامِ قَدْ ... وَافَتْ عَسَاكِرُهَا مَعَ السُّلْطَانِ

[21. /(208.)] So when you see the faction of Islam have assembled with their regiments alongside the Sulṭān,

فَهُنَاكَ فَاخْتَرِقِ الصُّفُوفَ وَلَا تَكُنْ ... بِالعَاجِزِ الوَانِي وَلَا الفَزْعَانِ

[22. /(209.)] Then at that point penetrate the ranks and do not be the one who is moaning weakling and do not be frightful

وَتَعَرَّ مِنْ ثَوْبَيْنِ مَنْ يَلْبَسْهُمَا ... يَلْقَى الرَّدَى بِمَذَمَّةٍ وَهَوَانِ

[23. /(210.)]Disrobe of two garments that cause whoever wears them to encounter ruin in dispraise and degradation:

ثَوْبٌ مِنَ الجَهْلِ المُرَكَّبِ فَوْقَهُ ... ثَوْبُ التَّعَصُّبِ بِئْسَتِ الثَّوْبَانِ

[24. /(211.)] A garment of compound ignorance above which is a garment of blind-fanaticism, how terrible are these two garments!

وَتَحَلَّ بِالإِنْصَافِ أَفْخَرَ حُلَّةٍ ... زِيْنَتْ بِهَا الأَعْطَافُ وَالْكَتِفَانِ

[25. /(212.)] Adorn yourself with fair objectivity, which is the most honorable apparel used to beautify the sides and shoulders.

وَاجْعَلْ شِعَارَكَ خَشْيَةَ الرَّحْمَنِ مَعْ ... نُصْحِ الرَّسُولِ فَحَبَّذَا الأَمْرَانِ

[26. /(213.)] Make your emblem the fear of al-Raḥmān along with genuineness for the Messenger (ﷺ), how commendable are these two matters!

وَتَمَسَّكَنَّ بِحَبْلِهِ وَبِوَحْيِهِ ... وَتَوَكَّلَنَّ حَقِيقَةَ التُّكْلَانِ

[27. /(214.)] And hold fast to his rope and his revelation, and place your reliance on Him with true dependency.

Synopsis of Lines 21-27

Muhammad Khalīl Harrās(رحمه الله) summarizes:

After prohibiting the person of truth from contending alone without troops or support — declaring that to be madness unbefitting for people of faith — then he commands him to not be spiritless or cowardly once the faction of truth have assembled with their battalions and taken their positions alongside the *Sulṭān*.[15] Rather, one is to storm the enemy ranks and plunge into the thick of danger without suffering from helplessness, whimpering, or dread of the adversary. He then commands him to disrobe of two garments that cause their wearer to eventuate in ruin and force him to drink from the goblet of degradation and humiliation. These two garments are: (1.) the garment of compounded ignorance and above that is (2.) the garment of fanaticism. These two garments are not found collectively upon any person except that they insert him into waves of falsehood and mazes of misguidance, beautifying the evil of his actions and the hideousness of his creed so that he believes it to be attractive. The meaning of compound ignorance is that a person believes something that is contrary

[15] T.N.: The meaning of the Sulṭān (lit. the authority/ ruler) in these lines is an allusion to the authority of the truth, as is evident from the subsequent explanations of the scholars.

to the truth whilst believing himself to be upon the truth. So he is ignorant of the truth, yet does not know that he is ignorant of it. This is more repugnant that simple ignorance which is a lack of knowledge about the truth, meaning that the mind is void of it. How appropriate is the poet's statement:

قال حَمِيرُ حَكِيمٍ توما *** لَوْ أَنْصَفَ الدَّهْرُ كُنْتُ أَرْكَبُ

فَإِنِّي جَاهِلٌ بَسِيطٌ *** وَصَاحِبِي جَاهِلٌ مُرَكَّبُ

"Wise Tom's donkey said: If the times were fair then I would be riding. For indeed I am simply ignorant while my owner is a compounded ignoramus."

After that, he ordered to adorn oneself with the garment of fairness, which is the most dazzling garment by which a person can ornament their shoulders and sides. The intent is that he treats his opponent objectively, not denying anything of the truth possessed by such a person nor the admissible relevance of some of his arguments. Instead, it is mandatory to mention both what is for and against them without condescension or denial. He is to adopt the immediate apparel of fearfulness of Allah (عَزَّوَجَلَّ) while skirmishing with these enemies in order to restrain him from violation and tyranny. He is to utilize the Messenger's advice to leave off (pointless) disputation and argumentation, for certainly that serves as a safety valve. He is to hold fast to Allah's unbreakable rope and clear revelation, depending on Him with true reliance, which is: surrendering one's affair to him while seeking his aid against his foes after exerting maximum effort in readying the means of victory and success.

21. Strength in Unity

فَإِذَا رَأَيْتَ عِصَابَةَ الإِسْلَامِ قَدْ ... وَافَتْ عَسَاكِرُهَا مَعَ السُّلْطَانِ

[21. /(208.)] So when you see the faction of Islam have assembled with their regiments alongside the Sulṭān,

Muhammad bin Sālih al 'Uthaymīn (رَحِمَهُ اللَّهُ) explains:

His saying, "*so when you see the 'iṣāba (i.e. faction) of Islām*" means: the people who are the *'iṣāba* of Islām, meaning those with group allegiance for it. His saying, "*...have assembled with their regiments alongside the Sulṭān,*" means that they have gathered with the *Sulṭān*, so then stand alongside them. For this reason he said, "*then at that point penetrate the ranks and do not be the one who is a whining weakling and do not be terrified.*"

Sālih al Fawzān (حفظه الله) explains:

He said: join with the people of truth an do not be on your own, independent with your opinion. So long as there is.a group from the people of truth, then join with them. This is a great wisdom, because uniting upon the truth is strength.

This entails an encouragement for unity and to not be alone individually. Even if the person is upon the truth, he should not be alone, rather, he should be with the *Jamā'ah*. (Allah) (تَبَارَكَ وَتَعَالَى) said:

﴿ وَلَا تَنَازَعُوا فَتَفْشَلُوا وَتَذْهَبَ رِيحُكُمْ ﴾

"And do not dispute and [thus] lose courage and [then] your strength would depart [al Anfāl: 46]

﴿ وَلَا تَكُونُوا كَالَّذِينَ تَفَرَّقُوا وَاخْتَلَفُوا مِن بَعْدِ مَا جَاءَهُمُ الْبَيِّنَاتُ ﴾

And do not be like the ones who became divided and differed after the clear proofs had come to them. [Aal 'Imrān: 105].

A benefit derived from this is that *jihād* must be alongside the ruler of the Muslims.

22. Do Not be Helpless, Complain or Be Fearful

فَهُنَاكَ فَاخْتَرِقِ الصُّفُوفَ وَلَا تَكُنْ ... بِالعَاجِزِ الوَانِي وَلَا الفَزْعَانِ

[22. /(209.)] Then at that point penetrate the ranks and do not a whining weakling and do not be frightful.

Muhammad bin Sālih al 'Uthaymīn (رحمه الله) explains:

Meaning that when once you have observed the people engaged in the confrontation and assembled for that purpose, "*then at that point penetrate the ranks*" and do not be a coward or be afraid so long as you are penetrating the ranks for Allah's sake while seeking His assistance. Be cautious against being stricken by defeatism, because once a person is stricken by defeatism and weakens, then his strengths lessen and he becomes unable to defend himself, let alone being able to advance against the people of falsehood.

23. Ridding Oneself of Loathsome Traits

وَتَعَرَّ مِنْ ثَوْبَيْنِ مَنْ يَلْبَسْهُمَا ... يَلْقَى الرَّدَى بِمَذَمَّةٍ وَهَوَانِ

[23. /(210.)]Disrobe of two garments that cause whoever wears them to encounter ruin in dispraise and degradation:

'Abd al-Rahmān al-Sa'dī (رحمه الله) explains:

This is an important advice for every student of knowledge, and moreover for every intelligent person.

Muhammad bin Sālih al 'Uthaymīn (رحمه الله) explains:

In his statement "*disrobe of two garments,*" then "*disrobe*" means to strip them off. At this point, he is ordering that we disrobe ourselves of two garments and he is clarifying that whoever wears these two garments will encounter ruin in a state of dispraise and degradation. He goes on to mention the first garment. He says:

24. Compound Ignorance & Blind Fanaticism

ثَوْبٌ مِنَ الجَهْلِ المُرَكَّبِ فَوْقَهُ ... ثَوْبُ التَّعَصُّبِ بِئْسَتِ الثَّوْبَانِ

[24. /(211.)] A garment of compound ignorance above which is a garment of blind-fanaticism, how terrible are these two garments!

Ahmad bin 'Isā al-Najdī (رحمه الله) *explains:*

Compound ignorance is conceptualizing something in a way that is contrary to its essence. It is that one's judgment ascertains something as being definite although that does not conform to its actuality. It is corrupt belief and compounded ignorance because it consists of a lack of knowledge about something while harboring a counterfactual belief about it. It is that one is ignorant of the truth, while being ignorant of his ignorance of it. Simple ignorance is simply a lack of knowledge.

'Abd al-Rahmān al-Sa'dī (رحمه الله) *explains:*

As for his statement, "*a garment of compound ignorance*," then it is that which is compounded of two things: (1.) perceiving something in a manner contrary to its reality, while (2.) claiming to have knowledge about it and being correct regarding it. As for simple ignorance, then it is that a person does not know while admitting their ignorance. This is less severe than the first type because the first person does not know, yet does not know that he does not know; whereas, the second type knows that he does not know. So it is befitting of you that whenever you are asked something that you do not know that you say: I do not know — even if you have the highest status amongst the people. Some have said: Indeed if you had said, "I don't know," then they would have taught you until you knew, however when you said "I know," while you did not, then they tested you until they knew that you did not know.

Sālih al Fawzān (حفظه الله) explains:

This is another advice. He says *"strip off the garment of ignorance and the garment of blind-fanaticism from yourself."* This is done by making the truth your ultimate objective as opposed to making the defense of your opinion as your goal. Likewise, strip away ignorance by learning knowledge, because ignorance is a fatal sickness.

The ignorant person is not suitable to debate the people of falsehood because he will ruin more than he repairs. Ignorance is a lack of knowing the truth and is divided into two categories. The first is compound ignorance. Compound ignorance is that one is ignorant, yet he is ignorant of the fact that he is ignorant. Instead, he imagines himself to be knowledgable. This is the most severe ignorance and is a calamity. This is what is termed as pretentiousness in our time, which is that a person claims knowledge without having any knowledge. The second type is simple ignorance, which is that someone does not know, but knows that they are ignorant. Therefore, if one knows that they are ignorant, then they will strive to learn.

Muhammad bin Sālih al 'Uthaymīn (رحمه الله) explains:

Compound ignorance is as such that when it a person has it as a trait, then he is deemed ignorant while not knowing that he is ignorant. That is because people are of three types:

The first: a knowledgeable person whose knowledge conforms to reality.

The second: one who supposes himself to be knowledgeable, yet he is ignorant.

The third: an ignorant person who absolutely does not know. As for the first type, then it is praiseworthy for a person to speak with knowledge that conforms to reality. As for the second, then that is the person of compounded ignorance. He does not know, while not knowing that he does not know. This is the worst category.

As for the third person, then he is ignorant, possessing simple ignorance that is not compounded. This is lighter in severity than the aforementioned type, yet is less than the status of the first, who is a knowledgeable person.

Every sort of calamity emanates from the ignoramus who possesses compound ignorance — the one who debates you without having knowledge. He generally speaks without knowledge. He speaks amongst the commoners without knowledge. He speaks to the scholars in a disputative manner without knowledge while seeing himself as being knowledgeable, as though he is the *Imām* of the *Imāms* and the chief of the scholars, and as though he is the scholar over the rulers, unapproachable in his status. Were you to investigate a matter with him, then he could not decipher his opposing wrist-bones from each other. He is from the most ignorant of Allah's servants. For this reason, we say that the person of compounded ignorance is the worst of the two types of ignoramuses: the first being the person of simple ignorance and the second is the one whose ignorance is compounded.

His statement *"over which is a garment of fanaticism"* is also somewhat unclear. It means fanaticism in favor of the falsehood or ignorance that he has. The fanatic is never dissuaded because of evidence because he believes that he is upon the truth, so he does not care about anyone.
He views it to be impossible to distance himself from what he is upon because he sees that as an indignity and thinks that if he recanted, then people who say that this is an ignorant man.

Doesn't he know that the Messenger (صَلَّى ٱللَّٰهُ عَلَيْهِ وَسَلَّمَ) sometimes issued a judgment and then realized that it should have been otherwise, upon which he would retract it. Likewise was the case with the Caliphs and the Imāms.

'Umar (رَضِيَ ٱللَّٰهُ عَنْهُ) wrote a letter pertaining judgeship to Abū Mūsā al Asha'rī (رَضِيَ ٱللَّٰهُ عَنْهُ) that is from the most tremendous and comprehensive of writings, to such an extent that Ibn al Qayyim (رَحِمَهُ ٱللَّٰهُ) made his book *'Ilām al Muwaqqi'īn* based upon 'Umar's communication to Abū Mūsā (رَضِيَ ٱللَّٰهُ عَنْهُ) pertaining judgeship. There are few books in Islam that are like it. He said to him:

لا يمنعْك من قضاءٍ قضيْتَ به اليوم فراجعت فيه نفسك ، وهديت فيه لرشدك ، تراجع فيه الحق ، فإنَّ الحقَّ قديمٌ ، ولا يُبْطِلُ الحقَّ شيءٌ ، فإنَّ مُرَاجَعَةَ الحقِّ خَيْرٌ مِنَ التَّمادي في الباطل

"Do not prevent yourself because a judgement that you rendered today — after which you introspected, resulting in being guided about it — do not let that prevent you from retracting in favor of the truth. For indeed, the truth is ancient and nothing can invalidate it. For certainly, returning to the truth is better than continuance in falsehood."

This is also a tremendous trial. Just as it affects the scholars in the issue of creed and religious fundamentals, it affects them in the issues of *fiqh*. So you find some scholars, especially those who blind-follow and have fanaticism for their *madhhab*, twisting the necks of the texts to agree with their *madhhab*.

Look at the books about differing, such as *al Mughnī* by al Muwaffaq Ibn Qudāma (رَحِمَهُ ٱللَّهُ) and *al Majmū' Sharḥ al Muhaddhab* by al-Nawawī (رَحِمَهُ ٱللَّهُ) and what is similar to them. You will find therein how some people are fanatical towards their *madhhab*, attempting to twist the necks of the texts to favor their particular school of *fiqh*. The cause of this trial is that people believe something before seeking evidence, thus he makes the evidence follow according to what he says and believes. It is mandatory to seek proof first, and then to believe accordingly. You are to make your belief and judgment follow according to the evidence, however the situation of fanaticism is confusing.

If someone were to say: how can you say this while the Christians say that the Muslims are fanatical for their religion? We say: that is praiseworthy fanaticism, rather it is mandatory, because they are not fanatical for it just because it is their religion, but because it is Allah's religion. This is similar to how we say that disputation is dispraised unless it is employed to affirm the truth or disprove falsehood.

These two garments — may Allah (عَزَّوَجَلَّ) protect us from them — are as such that when a person is afflicted with them, then he will be deprived of the receiving the truth. So you are to strip yourself from these two garments: compounded ignorance and fanaticism.

25. Objectivity & Fairness

وتَحَلَّ بِالإِنْصَافِ أَفْخَرَ حُلَّةٍ ... زِينَتْ بِهَا الأَعْطَافُ وَالْكِتْفَانِ

[25. /(212.)] Adorn yourself with objectivity, which is the honorable apparel used to beautify the sides and shoulders.

'Abd al-Rahmān al-Sa'dī (رحمه الله) explains:

As for his statement: "*adorn yourself with inṣāf* [i.e., objectivity], *which is the most honorable apparel*," then *inṣāf* is that you do towards people as you would like them to do unto you. Whoever incorporates that has adorned himself with objectivity, otherwise he is included in (Allah's) statement (تبارك وتعالى):

﴿ وَيْلٌ لِّلْمُطَفِّفِينَ (1) الَّذِينَ إِذَا اكْتَالُوا عَلَى النَّاسِ يَسْتَوْفُونَ (2) وَإِذَا كَالُوهُمْ أَو وَّزَنُوهُمْ يُخْسِرُونَ ﴾

"Woe to those who give less [than due], who, when they take a measure from people, take in full. But if they give by measure or by weight to them, they cause loss."[al Muṭaffifīn: 1]

This is general in its applicability to all interpersonal transactions and statements, etc.

Sālih al Fawzān (حفظه الله) explains:

Do not oppress people. Instead, be fair and give each person the rights that they deserve. This is a third advice.

Muhammad bin Sālih al 'Uthaymīn (رحمه الله) explains:

Then, after stripping these two garments off, he orders to adorn oneself with objectivity. His saying, "*adorn yourself with inṣaf* (i.e., fairness and objectivity)" means to clothe yourself with objectivity after disrobing from these two garments. His statement, "*inṣāf*" means justice, whether it is for or against you. This is just as Allah (تَبَارَكَ وَتَعَالَى) said:

﴿ يَا أَيُّهَا الَّذِينَ آمَنُوا كُونُوا قَوَّامِينَ بِالْقِسْطِ شُهَدَاءَ لِلَّهِ وَلَوْ عَلَىٰ أَنفُسِكُمْ أَوِ الْوَالِدَيْنِ وَالْأَقْرَبِينَ ﴾

"O you who have believed, be persistently standing firm in justice, witnesses for Allah, even if it be against yourselves or parents and relatives." [al-Nisā': 135]

From testifying against oneself is that a person is just with their opponent. So when the truth is clear, then it is mandatory on him to follow the truth, and when his opponent says something that entails truth and falsehood, then it is mandatory that he accepts the truth while rejecting falsehood. And it is not allowed for him to reject his entire statement.

26. Fearing Allah & Genuineness for the Messenger

وَاجْعَلْ شِعَارَكَ خَشْيَةَ الرَّحْمنِ مَعْ ... نُصْحِ الرَّسُولِ فَحَبَّذَا الأَمْرَانِ

[26. /(213.)] Make your emblem the fear of al-Raḥmān along with genuineness for the Messenger, how commendable are these two matters!

ʿAbd al-Raḥmān al-Sa'dī (رَحِمَهُ ٱللَّهُ) explains:

This statement of his: "*Make your immediate clothing consist of the fear of al-Raḥmān,*" is the basis of actions, whereas, "*along with genuineness for the Messenger, how commendable are these two*" is the basis of knowledge. This is because human completion is by way of knowledge and action. *Shi'ār* is any clothing that is directly over the body.

Sālih al Fawzān (حفظه الله) explains:

When your *Shi'ār* becomes the fear of al-Raḥmān and genuineness towards the Messenger (صَلَّى ٱللَّهُ عَلَيْهِ وَسَلَّمَ), then you will not be defeated, so long as Allah allows.

Sālih al Fawzān (حفظه الله) explains:

You are to make your *shi'ār* (i.e., slogan, banner, or closest apparel) to be fearfulness from Allah (عَزَّ وَجَلَّ), not coming to your own defense. As such, the Prophet (صَلَّى ٱللَّهُ عَلَيْهِ وَسَلَّمَ) did not exact retribution for his own self, rather, he only became defensive for Allah's sake, when Allah's sanctities were violated, at which point he would issue severe reprimand accordingly.

As for his statement, "*along with having genuineness for the Messenger*" means so long as one is true to the Prophet (صَلَّى ٱللَّٰهُ عَلَيْهِ وَسَلَّمَ), which is done by following him.

27. Hold Fast & Place Your Trust in Allah

وَتَمَسَّكَنَّ بِحَبْلِهِ وَبِوَحْيِهِ ... وَتَوَكَّلَنَّ حَقِيقَةَ التُّكْلَانِ

[27. /(214.)] And hold fast to his rope and his revelation, and place your reliance on Him with true dependency.

'Abd al-Rahmān al-Sa'dī (رَحِمَهُ ٱللَّٰهُ) explains:

In his statement: "*hold fast to His rope and His revelation*," the conjunction "*and*" denotes that these two things are synonymous. "*And place reliance on Him, with a true dependency*" *Al-Tawakkul* is genuine reliance on Allah (عَزَّ وَجَلَّ) in facilitating benefit and repelling harm, while having good thoughts that He will facilitate what you relied upon Him regarding.

Muhammad bin Sālih al 'Uthaymīn (رَحِمَهُ ٱللَّٰهُ) explains:

Meaning hold fast to Allah's rope as Allah (تَبَارَكَ وَتَعَالَىٰ) said:

﴿وَاعْتَصِمُوا بِحَبْلِ اللَّهِ جَمِيعًا وَلَا تَفَرَّقُوا﴾

"And hold firmly to the rope of Allah all together and do not become divided." [Aal 'Imrān: 103]

His saying, "*and His revelation*" means Allah's revelation to His Messenger (صَلَّىٰ ٱللَّهُ عَلَيْهِ وَسَلَّمَ).

His saying, "*and place your reliance on Him with true dependency*" means: depend upon Allah (عَزَّوَجَلَّ). This is because placing one's reliance upon Allah (عَزَّوَجَلَّ) is to have genuine dependency that He will facilitate what is beneficial and repel whatever is harmful while one maintains trust in Him and utilizes the beneficial means.

V. The Status & Description of the Truth
Synopsis of Lines 28-33:

28. The Truth is an Attribute of Allah & He Alone Guides to It

29. Allah is Upon the Straight Path of Truth

30. The Truth is Victorious & Trialled

31. Trialling Distinguishes Allah's Faction from Those Warring with Him

32. You Win Some, You Lose Some

33. The Final Outcome will Always Favor the Righteous

V. The Description of the Truth

فَالحَقُّ وَصْفُ الرَّبِّ وَهْوَ صِرَاطُهُ الـ ... هَادِي إِلَيْهِ لِصَاحِبِ الإِيْمَانِ

[28. /(215.)] For al Ḥaqq is a description of al-Rabb and it is His guiding path to Him for the possessor of faith.

وَهْوَ الصِّرَاطُ عَلَيْهِ رَبُّ العَرْشِ أَيْـ ... ضاً، ذَا وَذَا قَدْ جَاءَ فِي القُرْآنِ

[29. /(216.)] It is also the path that the Lord of the throne is upon — both this and that have come in the Qurān.

وَالحَقُّ مَنْصُورٌ وَمُمْتَحَنٌ فَلَا ... تَعْجَبْ فَهَذِي سُنَّةُ الرَّحْمَنِ

[30. /(217.)] The truth is aided and tested so do not be amazed, for this is the way of al-Raḥmān.

وَبِذَاكَ يَظْهَرُ حِزْبُهُ مِنْ حَرْبِهِ ... وَلِأَجْلِ ذَاكَ النَّاسُ طَائِفَتَانِ

[31. /(218.)] By way of that, His ḥizb becomes distinct from those warring with Him. And for that reason people are of two parties.

وَلِأَجْلِ ذَاكَ الحَرْبُ بَيْنَ الرُّسْلِ وَالْـ ... كُفَّارِ مُذْ قَامَ الوَرَى سِجْلَانِ

[32. /(219.)] And on account of that warring transpired between the Messengers and the unbelievers since humankind's beginning, alternating (between victory and defeat).

لَكِنَّمَا العُقْبَى لِأَهْلِ الحَقِّ إِنْ ... فَاتَتْ هُنَا كَانَ لَدَى الدَّيَّانِ

[33. /(220.)] However, the final outcome will favor the people of truth. And if that does not happen here then it will happen upon meeting with al Dayyān [i.e., Allah, the Divine Judge].

Synopsis of Lines 28-33

Muhammad Khalīl Harrās(رَحِمَهُ ٱللَّهُ) summarizes:

Having invited him to adhering to the truth, maintaining resoluteness thereupon, and contending in its defense, he then wanted to show the status of that truth and that it is worthy of every sacrifice exerted in its path. So he mentioned that the truth has a number of meanings. One of them is that it is a Divine Attribute of *al-Rabb*, as Allah (تَبَارَكَ وَتَعَالَىٰ) said:

﴿ يَوْمَئِذٍ يُوَفِّيهِمُ اللَّهُ دِينَهُمُ الْحَقَّ وَيَعْلَمُونَ أَنَّ اللَّهَ هُوَ الْحَقُّ الْمُبِينُ ﴾

"That Day, Allah will pay them in full their deserved recompense)their dīn), And they will know that Allah, He is the Manifest Truth." [al-Nūr: 25].

Another meaning is that it is Allah's path to which He guides whomever He wills of His slaves — from the adherents of faith and guidance. This is as Allah (تَبَارَكَ وَتَعَالَىٰ) stated:

﴿ أَفَمَن يَهْدِي إِلَى الْحَقِّ أَحَقُّ أَن يُتَّبَعَ أَمَّن لَّا يَهِدِّي إِلَّا أَن يُهْدَىٰ ﴾

"So is He who guides to the truth more worthy to be followed or he who guides not unless he is guided?" [Yunus: 35].

Likewise, He (تَبَارَكَ وَتَعَالَىٰ) said:

﴿ فَهَدَى اللَّهُ الَّذِينَ آمَنُوا لِمَا اخْتَلَفُوا فِيهِ مِنَ الْحَقِّ بِإِذْنِهِ ۗ وَاللَّهُ يَهْدِي مَن يَشَاءُ إِلَىٰ صِرَاطٍ مُّسْتَقِيمٍ ﴾

"And Allah guided those who believed to the truth concerning that over which they had differed, by His permission. And Allah guides whom He wills to a straight path." [al Baqara: 213].

Another meaning is that it is the path about which Allah (عَزَّوَجَلَّ) informed us that He is upon. This is as He (تَبَارَكَ وَتَعَالَى) said:

﴿إِنَّ رَبِّي عَلَىٰ صِرَاطٍ مُّسْتَقِيمٍ﴾

"Verily, my Lord is on the Straight Path (the truth)." [Hūd: 56].

Meaning pertaining His statements and actions, so His statement is truth, direction, genuine advice, and guidance. His actions are wisdom, justice, mercy, and benefit.

Then he also mentioned that from the truth's great status is that it is victorious and that the end result is in its favor. However it is trialled and tested by way of the antagonism and disturbance of falsehood.

Allah's way has always been like this so that Allah's faction could be distinguished from Shayṭān's and so that the battle between truth and falsehood between Allah's Messengers and their disbelieving enemies could continuously alternate in fortunes, after which the end result ultimately favors the pious. This is just as He (تَبَارَكَ وَتَعَالَى) said:

﴿وَالْعَاقِبَةُ لِلتَّقْوَىٰ﴾

"And the [best] outcome is for [those of] righteousness."[ṬaHa: 132].

Also, He (تَبَارَكَ وَتَعَالَى) said, conveying what was spoken on the tongue of Moses:

﴿ وَالْعَاقِبَةُ لِلْمُتَّقِينَ ﴾

"And the [best] outcome is for the righteous."[al 'Arāf: 128].

If this end escapes the believers in this world then it will be in store for them with Allah (عَزَّوَجَلَّ) who will fulfill it for them on Judgment Day, whereupon He will exact retribution on their behalf against the oppressive transgressors.

28. The Truth is an Attribute of Allah and He Alone Guides to It

فَالحَقُّ وَصْفُ الرَّبِّ وَهْوَ صِرَاطُهُ الـ... هَادِي إِلَيْهِ لِصَاحِبِ الإِيْمَانِ

[28./(215.)] For al Ḥaqq is a description of al-Rabb and it is His path guiding to Him for the possessor of faith.

Ahmad bin 'Isā al-Najdī (رحمه الله) explains:

As for the syntactic derivation of [the word] ***ṣirāṭ***, then what is known is that it originates from the meaning of easily swallowing something for ingestion. So a path is called a *ṣirāṭ* because it passes its traverser through it. The *ṣirāṭ* is that which gathers five attributes: (1.) that it be a straight path; (2.) easy to traverse; (3.) well-travelled; (4.) of an accommodating width; (5.) eventuating in one's destination. Therefore a crooked path is not called a *ṣirāṭ*; nor is a cumbersome, difficult one; nor is one that is obstructed or disconnected. Whoever reflects upon the contextualization of *ṣirāṭ* in (Arabic) dialects and usages will realize that. They [i.e., the Arabs] construe the word [i.e., *ṣirāṭ*] on the syntactic scale of *fi'āl* because it is envelops its traverser just as the throat envelops something being gulped. This syntactic scale is commonly used for things that envelop other things, such as: *liḥāf* (blanket), ***khimār*** (cloaking-scarf), *ridā'* (cloak), *ghiṭā'* (covering), and *firāsh* (mattress). This (explanation) was given by the author of the poetry [i.e., Ibn al Qayyim (رَحِمَهُ ٱللَّهُ)] as a benefit.[16]

'Abd al-Rahmān al-Sa'dī (رَحِمَهُ ٱللَّهُ) explains:

"*Al Ḥaqq is the attribute of al-Rabb*" Meaning it a description of His essence. Therefore, ***al Ḥaqq*** is from His Names. "*Also, it His path that guides the possessor of faith to Him.*" Meaning that Allah's path, which is His religion and His law, is described as being the truth. It guides the possessor of faith to Allah (عَزَّوَجَلَّ), just as Allah (تَبَارَكَ وَتَعَالَىٰ) said:

﴿ وَأَنَّ هَٰذَا صِرَاطِي مُسْتَقِيمًا فَاتَّبِعُوهُ ۖ وَلَا تَتَّبِعُوا السُّبُلَ فَتَفَرَّقَ بِكُمْ عَن سَبِيلِهِ ﴾

"And, [moreover], this is My path, which is straight, so follow it; and do not follow [other] ways, for you will be separated from His way."[al An'ām: 153]

Muhammad bin Sālih al 'Uthaymīn (رَحِمَهُ ٱللَّهُ) explains:

As for His statement, "*al Ḥaqq is the attribute of al-Rabb [i.e. the Nurturing Lord]*" then Allah is *al Ḥaqq* and the truth is His Attribute, due to Allah's saying (تَبَارَكَ وَتَعَالَىٰ):

---

16 see Ibn al Qayyim's Badā'i al Fawā'id vol. 2, p. 16

﴿ ذَٰلِكَ بِأَنَّ اللَّهَ هُوَ الْحَقُّ ﴾

"That is because Allah, He is the Truth" [al Ḥajj: 6]

The truth is anything verified that is in conformity to reality. When that thing is information it is called *al-ṣidq* (the truth) and when it is something in demand or something created, then it is called benefit.

As for his statement, "*and it is the path guiding to Him for the person of faith,*" then it is the path leading to Him, because Allah described the path leading to Him as being truth. He (تَبَارَكَ وَتَعَالَى) said:

﴿ قُلِ اللَّهُ يَهْدِي لِلْحَقِّ ۗ أَفَمَن يَهْدِي إِلَى الْحَقِّ أَحَقُّ أَن يُتَّبَعَ أَمَّن لَّا يَهِدِّي إِلَّا أَن يُهْدَىٰ ﴾

"Say: Allah guides to the truth. So is He who guides to the truth more worthy to be followed or he who guides not unless he is guided?" [Yunus: 35].

So the path — meaning the religion — is described as the truth, due to Allah's statement (تَبَارَكَ وَتَعَالَى):

﴿ يَوْمَئِذٍ يُوَفِّيهِمُ اللَّهُ دِينَهُمُ الْحَقَّ وَيَعْلَمُونَ أَنَّ اللَّهَ هُوَ الْحَقُّ الْمُبِينُ ﴾

"That Day, Allah will pay them in full their deserved recompense (their dīn), and they will know that Allah, He is the Manifest Truth." [al-Nūr: 25]

So He is al Ḥaqq, and He is the Guide to the truth, and His path is likewise the truth. So these are three matters. So Allah (عَزَّوَجَلَّ) is al Ḥaqq — the truth being His attribute. So He guides His servants, directing and leading them to the truth; and His path leading to Him is the truth. So the Messenger (صَلَّىٰٱللَّهُعَلَيْهِوَسَلَّمَ) is truth, the Paradise is truth, and the Hellfire is truth because everything affirmed that conforms to reality is truth.

29. Allah is Upon the Straight Path of Truth

وَهُوَ الصِّرَاطُ عَلَيْهِ رَبُّ العَرْشِ أَيْـ ... ـضاً، ذَا وَذَا قَدْ جَاءَ فِي القُرآنِ

[29. /(216.)] It is also the path that the Lord of the throne is upon — both this and that have come in the Qurān.

'Abd al-Rahmān al-Sa'dī (رَحِمَهُ ٱللَّهُ) explains:

As for His statement, "*and it is the Path which the Rabb of the throne is upon*," then this is like what was stated by Hūd:

﴿ إِنَّ رَبِّي عَلَىٰ صِرَاطٍ مُّسْتَقِيمٍ ﴾

"Verily, my Lord is on the Straight Path (the truth)."[Hūd: 56]

This is an evidence for the affirmation of Divine Wisdom, meaning: Allah (عَزَّوَجَلَّ) legislated the laws, issued the commandments, created creation, and arranged reward and punishment for an amazing wisdom which is described as being the clear truth. The *Ṣirāṭ* is the path. However it is not called a *Ṣirāṭ* until it combines five descriptive traits, which are that it is: straight, easy, followed, vast, and that it leads to the destination in the shortest distance. A crooked path is not called a *ṣirāṭ*, neither is a difficult and hard one, nor is one that is blocked and disconnected. Whoever reflects over the Arabs' speech will realize that.

Muhammad bin Sālih al 'Uthaymīn (رَحِمَهُ ٱللَّهُ) explains:

His statement. "*and it is the path*" means that the truth is also the *Ṣirāṭ* [i.e., the path]. As for his statement, "*that the Lord of the Throne is upon*," then the evidence of that is His statement (تَبَارَكَ وَتَعَالَىٰ):

﴿إِنَّ رَبِّي عَلَىٰ صِرَاطٍ مُّسْتَقِيمٍ﴾

"Verily, my Lord is on the Straight Path (the truth)."[Hūd: 56]

Meaning that it is a straight path without any crookedness. So you will find that everything Allah (عَزَّوَجَلَّ) legislated and created to be in total conformity to the truth because Allah (عَزَّوَجَلَّ) is upon a straight path. As for his statement that "that has come in the Qurān," then where has it come in the Qurān that Allah (عَزَّوَجَلَّ) is upon the straight path? The answer: It has come in His statement (تَبَارَكَ وَتَعَالَىٰ):

﴿إِنَّ رَبِّي عَلَىٰ صِرَاطٍ مُّسْتَقِيمٍ﴾

"Verily, my Lord is on the Straight Path (the truth)."[Hūd: 56]

30. The Truth is Victorious & Trialled

وَالحَقُّ مَنْصُورٌ وَمُمْتَحَنٌ فَلَا ... تَعْجَبْ فَهَذِي سُنَّةُ الرَّحْمَنِ

[30. /(217.)] The truth is victorious and trialled so do not be shocked, for this is the way of al-Raḥmān.

'Abd al-Rahmān al-Sa'dī (رحمه الله) explains:

Once you have understood this and know that he who holds fast to it is upon the truth, then know that "*the truth is victorious*" in the end, "*and trialed*" in the beginning, "*so do not be amazed, this is the way of al-Raḥmān.*"

Muhammad bin Sālih al 'Uthaymīn (رحمه الله) explains:

As for his statement, "*the truth is victorious and trialled,*" then O Allah! Give victory to the truth and make it victorious through us. The truth is inexorably victorious due to Allah's saying (تَبَارَكَ وَتَعَالَى):

﴿ إِنَّا لَنَنصُرُ رُسُلَنَا وَالَّذِينَ آمَنُوا فِي الْحَيَاةِ الدُّنْيَا وَيَوْمَ يَقُومُ الْأَشْهَادُ ﴾

"Verily, We will indeed make victorious Our Messengers and those who believe in this world's life and on the Day when the witnesses will stand forth"[Ghāfir: 51]

However trialling must happen. As such, then he said, "*and it is trialled so do not be shocked*" meaning do not disapprove of Allah (عَزَّوَجَلَّ) trialling the people of truth with tribulations as a test.

Don't you see that gold does not become pure unless it is first subjected to fire which melts it and removes its impurity? So trialling must occur. The evidence for that is reality and the revealed religion.

As for reality, then look at the trials that happened to the Prophet! There were tremendous trials in the beginning of the da'wah and at the end. What happened to him in Makkah? What happened to him in Ṭā'if? What happened to him in al Madīnah? Wasn't his face split open and weren't his cuspid teeth broken? The answer is of course that happened. So trialling must happen.

As for what is found in that regard in the revelation, then Allah (تَبَارَكَ وَتَعَالَىٰ) said:

﴿ وَكَذَٰلِكَ جَعَلْنَا لِكُلِّ نَبِيٍّ عَدُوًّا مِّنَ الْمُجْرِمِينَ ﴾

"And thus have We made for every prophet an enemy from among the criminals." [al Furqān: 31]

Do you think that your enemy will sleep without trying to finish you off? Never. However, read what comes after this sentence:

﴿ وَكَفَىٰ بِرَبِّكَ هَادِيًا وَنَصِيرًا ﴾

"But sufficient is your Lord as a guide and a helper." [al Furqān: 31]

This is because when the enemy initiates a surprise attack to do away with what you have come with of the religion and to distract you, then he is confronted with guidance. "*Your Lord is sufficient as a Guide*." So no matter how much the enemy tries to mislead people from Allah's path, then Allah (عَزَّوَجَلَّ) is the Guide. No matter how much the enemy tries to do away with you by military might, then he is confronted by Divine Support. "*And your Lord is sufficient as a Guide and Helper.*"

As for his statement, "*then do not be shocked, for this is the way of al-Raḥmān,*" then we have already proven with religious textual proof as well as with reality that this is al-Raḥmān's way. So trialling must occur. For that reason we see in our daily or yearly lives that when does a person prove successful? When they excel during exam time. So trialling must take place.

Sālih al Fawzān (حفظه الله) explains:

If the people of truth encounter a calamity or tragedy, then do not allow this to unravel your determination or your drive. The truth is victorious and trialled. If the truth was always victorious, then no person would have any distinct virtue. However, from Allah's way is that He alternates fortunes between the servants. During his conflict with the unbelievers, the Messenger (صَلَّى ٱللَّٰهُ عَلَيْهِ وَسَلَّمَ) was sometimes victorious. At other times he encountered trialling as occurred during Uḥud, Ḥunayn and on other occasions.

The truth may be afflicted by way of its people having a defect, not because of their being a defect in the truth. The defect is only in the people of truth, so they are afflicted by their enemies. If this happens, then do not allow that to undo your determination or make you lose interest in the truth. Instead, be firm and patient; and repair the defect within yourself, because this particular matter did not afflict you or you associates except because of some deficiency within yourselves.

﴿أَوَلَمَّا أَصَابَتْكُم مُّصِيبَةٌ قَدْ أَصَبْتُم مِّثْلَيْهَا قُلْتُمْ أَنَّىٰ هَٰذَا ۖ قُلْ هُوَ مِنْ عِندِ أَنفُسِكُمْ﴾

"(What is the matter with you?) When a single disaster smites you, although you smote (your enemies) with one twice as great, you say: 'From where does this come to us?' Say (to them), 'It is from yourselves (because of your evil deeds).'" [Aal 'Imrān: 165].

This is a principle: the truth is not always victorious, and victory does not always favor the people of truth [in this life]. This is from the door of affliction and being trialled. So it is upon you to be patient and anticipate deliverance. Do not despair.

﴿وَلَن يَجْعَلَ اللَّهُ لِلْكَافِرِينَ عَلَى الْمُؤْمِنِينَ سَبِيلًا﴾

"And never will Allah grant to the disbelievers a way (to triumph) over the believers." [Al-Nisā': 141]

31. Trialling Distinguishes Allah's Faction from Those Warring with Him

وَبِذَاكَ يَظْهَرُ حِزْبُهُ مِنْ حَرْبِهِ ... وَلِأَجْلِ ذَاكَ النَّاسُ طَائِفَتَانِ

[31. /(218.)] By that His ḥizb becomes distinct from those warring with Him. And for that reason people are of two parties.

'Abd al-Raḥmān al-Sa'dī (رحمه الله) explains:

He said: "*By way of that*" trialling "*His ḥizb*" — and His allies, "*becomes distinct from those warring against Him*" and enemies.

"*And for that reason*" meaning trialling, "*people are of two parties.*" Had it not been for trialling to distinguish between the obedient and the disobedient, then that would not happen.

Muhammad bin Sālih al 'Uthaymīn (رَحِمَهُ ٱللَّهُ) explains:

His saying, "*by that*" means by way of the truth being victorious and trialled, His *ḥizb* becomes distinct from those warring with Him. The warring party is at odds with what has come of revelation and it is at odds with Allah's religion, whereas the *ḥizb* is the party of Allah that comes to the defense of Allah's religion and so Allah (عَزَّوَجَلَّ) aids them as a result. So he is saying: do not be shocked because of that. For indeed, this is Allah's way so that that Allah's faction can be distinct from those warring with Allah. If that were not the case, then the people would be a single nation and Allah's faction would not be distinguished from those warring with Him. For the reason that the truth is victorious and trialled the people become two separate factions, however, the final outcome in in favor of the people of truth as has preceded in Allah's statement (تَبَارَكَ وَتَعَالَىٰ):

﴿إِنَّا لَنَنصُرُ رُسُلَنَا وَالَّذِينَ آمَنُوا فِي الْحَيَاةِ الدُّنْيَا وَيَوْمَ يَقُومُ الْأَشْهَادُ يَوْمَ لَا يَنفَعُ الظَّالِمِينَ مَعْذِرَتُهُمْ ۖ وَلَهُمُ اللَّعْنَةُ وَلَهُمْ سُوءُ الدَّارِ﴾

"Verily, We will indeed make victorious Our Messengers and those who believe in this world's life and on the Day when the witnesses will stand forth"[Ghāfir: 51-52]

Sālih al Fawzān (حفظه الله) explains:

This is the wisdom: to distinguish the party of al-Raḥmān from the party of al-Shayṭān — who are at war with Allah. He distinguishes between these two. Otherwise, if victory was always in favor of the believers, there would be do distinction and all people would enter into the religion out of desiring this victory and dignity.

32.You Win Some, You Lose Some

وَلِأَجْلِ ذَاكَ الحَرْبُ بَيْنَ الرُّسْلِ وَالْـ... كُفَّارِ مُذْ قَامَ الوَرَى سِجْلَانِ

[32. /(219.)] And on account of that warring transpired between the Messengers and the unbelievers since humankind's beginning, alternating (between victory and defeat).

'Abd al-Rahmān al-Sa'dī (رحمه الله) explains:

This is just as Abū Sufyān bin Ḥarb said to Heraclius: "The war between us and them is *sijāl* — he takes some of ours and we take some of his" in reference to the Prophet (صلى الله عليه وسلم). This was before Abu Sufyān (رضي الله عنه) accepted Islam.

Sālih al Fawzān (حفظه الله) explains:

Sijlān means that one day [i.e., skirmish] is in their favor, whereas another is against them. However, the final outcome does not continue perpetually, but rather it dissipates and the final outcome is constantly and always for the pious.

33. The Final Outcome will Always Favor the Righteous

لَكِنَّمَا العُقْبَى لِأَهْلِ الحَقِّ إِنْ ... فَاتَتْ هُنَا كَانَ لَدَى الدَّيَّانِ

[33. /(220.)] However, the final outcome will favor the people of truth. And if that does not happen here then it will happen upon meeting with al Dayyān [i.e., Allah, the Divine Judge].

'Abd al-Rahmān al-Sa'dī (رحمه الله) explains:

He said: "*However the final result...*" to the end (of the sentence). So it is certain that the people of truth are victorious. They might achieve victory in this world, otherwise they will definitely have it in the hereafter.

Muhammad bin Sālih al 'Uthaymīn (رحمه الله) explains:

He spoke the truth here. Allah (تَبَارَكَ وَتَعَالَى) said:

﴿ فَاصْبِرْ ۖ إِنَّ الْعَاقِبَةَ لِلْمُتَّقِينَ ﴾

"So be patient; indeed, the [best] outcome is for the righteous." [Hūd: 49]

Meaning: be patient with what reaches you of abuse, adversity, hostility, and hatred. Be patient, "*Indeed the final outcome favors the pious.*"

Allah (عَزَّوَجَلَّ) has spoken the truth. By Allah! Who will the final outcome favor? The Messenger (صَلَّىٱللَّهُعَلَيْهِوَسَلَّمَ) defeated the chieftains of Quraysh and those of them who survived became the defenders of Islām. They became leaders in Islam — *mujāhidīn* in Allah's path. Don't forget Khālid bin al Walīd, 'Ikrimah bin Abī Jahl, and others besides them (رَضِيَٱللَّهُعَنْهُمْ).

The message spread until it went beyond the Arabian peninsula to the Earth's East, its West, its North, and its South. So the final outcome was in whose favor? Was it in the favor of Abū Jahl and his people, or was it in favor of Allah's Messenger Muḥammad (صَلَّىٱللَّهُعَلَيْهِوَسَلَّمَ)? The answer is that it was in favor of the second without any doubt.

Despite that, he goes on to say at this point, "*if that escapes you here, then it will happen upon meeting al-Dayyān (i.e., Allah the Divine Judge).*" Meaning that if victory escapes you in the temporal world then it will be with Allah in the Hereafter. For this reason, He (تَبَارَكَوَتَعَالَىٰ) said:

﴿إِنَّا لَنَنصُرُ رُسُلَنَا وَالَّذِينَ آمَنُوا فِي الْحَيَاةِ الدُّنْيَا وَيَوْمَ يَقُومُ الْأَشْهَادُ﴾

"Verily, We will indeed make victorious Our Messengers and those who believe in this world's life and on the Day when the witnesses will stand forth"[Ghāfir: 51]

Imagine that one of the du'āt undertakes inviting to Allah's religion, clarifying the falsity of what the people of falsehood or upon, only to be killed before he completes what he intended. So at this point, victory has escaped him in the temporal world, however the final outcome will be in his favor in the hereafter.

If he misses out on it in this world, then he will find it in the hereafter.

The final outcome is in favor of the people of truth. If it escapes them in the temporal world they will find it with *al-Dayyān* — with Allah (عَزَّوَجَلَّ). So the final outcome favors them no matter what, either in both this world and the hereafter, or only in the hereafter. As for being deprived of victory entirely, then that is something impossible as has preceded in the aforementioned verse.

However, I have constantly repeated that victory is not victory of the individual person, but rather it is victory of the path that he is traversing. If it were imagined that Allah (عَزَّوَجَلَّ) concludes a person's life in this world before he witnesses first-hand victory — meaning the victory of what he was upon — then certainly his methodology will be victorious afterwards and will be established, so long as it is the methodology that Allah (عَزَّوَجَلَّ) has made specifically for his worshipful servants.

For this reason, we say that the Muslims' victory after the death of Allah's Messenger was a victory for the Messenger (صَلَّىٱللَّهُعَلَيْهِوَسَلَّمَ), even though it was after his death. This is proven by what Heraclius, the Roman emperor said when Abū Sufyān reported to him what the Messenger of Allah (صَلَّىٱللَّهُعَلَيْهِوَسَلَّمَ) was engaged in of the invitation to the truth. Heraclius said to Abu Sufyan, "If what you are saying is true, then he will come to rule what is under these two feet of mine."

But did the Messenger (صَلَّىٱللَّهُعَلَيْهِوَسَلَّمَ) come to rule what was under his feet? The answer is that yes he did, however he did not do so personally. Instead, he did so through his religion and his methodology.

VI. The Two Migrations (Lines 34-39)
Synopsis of Lines 34-39:

34. Two Mandatory Migrations

35. The First Migration: Sincerity

36. The Definition of Sincerity

37. Sincerity Spares a Person from Shirk

38: Migration to the Prophet

39. The Reality of The Second Migration

VI. The Two Migrations (Lines 34-39)

وَاجْعَل لِقَلْبِكَ هِجْرَتَيْنِ وِلَا تَنَمْ ... فَهُمَا عَلَى كُلِّ امْرِئٍ فَرْضَانِ

[34. /(221.)] Make your heart embark upon two migrations and do not fall asleep. For certainly they are mandatory for every person.

فَالهِجْرَةِ الأُوْلَى إِلَى الرَّحْمَنِ بِالْـ ... إِخْلَاصِ فِي سِرٍّ وَفِي إِعْلَانِ

[35. /(222.)] The first is the migration to al-Raḥmān by way of sincerity in private and in public.

فَالْقَصْدُ وَجْهُ اللهِ بِالْأَقْوَالِ وَالْ ... أَعْمَالِ وَالْطَّاعَاتِ وَالْشُّكْرَانِ

[36. /(223.)] So the intention is to be for Allah's Face, by all words, deeds, acts of obedience, and gratitude.

فَبِذَاكَ يَنْجُو العَبْدُ مِنْ إِشْرَاكِهِ ... وَيَصِيرُ حَقًّا عَابِدَ الرَّحْمَنِ

[37. /(224.)] By doing that the worshipful-slave is spared from ascribing partners to him, and in doing so becomes a true worshipful-slave for al-Raḥmān.

والهِجْرَةُ الأُخْرَى اِلَى الْمَبْعُوثِ بِالْـ ... حَقِّ المُبِينِ وَوَاضِحِ البُرْهَانِ

[38. /(225.)] The other migration is to the one who was dispatched with the unambiguous truth and clear proof.

فَيَدُورُ مَعَ قَوْلِ الرَّسُولِ وَفِعْلِهِ ... نَفْيًا وَإِثْبَاتًا بِلَا رَوَغَانِ

[39. /(226.)] So he is centered upon the axis of the Messenger's statements and actions pertaining what is negated and what is affirmed, without any shiftiness.

Synopsis of Lines 34-39

Muḥammad Khalīl Harrās (رَحِمَهُ ٱللَّهُ) *summarizes:*

It is compulsory for any pursuer of salvation who is genuine in having goodwill for himself to undertake these two phenomenal migrations in a state of strength and determination without laziness or fatigue. For indeed, there is no rectitude or salvation for the worshipper except by way of them both. Therefore, undertaking them is a definite obligation upon every person.

As for the first migration, then it is his migration to Allah (عَزَّوَجَلَّ) by way of sincerity pertaining worshipping him in private and in public. He is not to intend anything save Allah's face in every statement, action, obedient act, and instance of thankfulness that emerges from himself, so as to be safe from assigning counterparts. Thus he renders his worship in its proper place as pertains validity and acceptability.

As for the other migration, then it is his migration to the Messenger (صَلَّىٰٱللَّهُعَلَيْهِوَسَلَّمَ) by way of good emulation and following, without opposing his commandments and rebelling against his judgments. Thus, he aligns himself with his statements and actions as regards negation and affirmation. So he does not affirm what the Messenger (صَلَّىٰٱللَّهُعَلَيْهِوَسَلَّمَ) negated and does not negate what the Messenger (صَلَّىٰٱللَّهُعَلَيْهِوَسَلَّمَ) affirmed. He does so without inclining to whimsicality, confused stumbling into misinterpretation, or following *Shayṭān*.

34. Two Mandatory Migrations

وَاجْعَل لِقَلْبِكَ هِجْرَتَيْنِ وِلَا تَنَمْ ... فَهُمَا عَلَى كُلِّ امْرِئٍ فَرْضَانِ

[34./(221.)] Make your heart embark upon two migrations and do not fall asleep. For certainly they are mandatory for every person.

Ahmad bin 'Isā al-Najdī (رَحِمَهُ ٱللَّٰهُ) explains:

The author of the poetry then commences in mentioning the two migrations. The first migration is towards Allah (عَزَّوَجَلَّ) by way of sincerity in actions and having an orientation focused on Him by implementation of His commandments and abstention from His prohibitions. The second migration is to the Messenger (صَلَّىٱللَّهُعَلَيْهِوَسَلَّمَ) by way of emulating him, giving his statements precedence in what is minor and major, and by abandoning the statements of others in favor of his. The author has a book that he named The Journey of the Two Migrations and the Path of Two Felicities [*Safar al Hijratayn wa Ṭarīq al-Sa'ādatayn* — most commonly known as *Ṭarīq al Hijratayn*] in which he has produced that which needs nothing supplementary, so refer to it if you wish.

'Abd al-Rahmān al-Sa'dī (رَحِمَهُ ٱللَّٰهُ) explains:

His statement: "*Make your heart embark on two migrations*" meaning constantly and always. "*And do not go to sleep*" on any night until you have brought them to mind and trained yourself to embark upon them. There are innumerable advantages and benefits in doing so. "*For certainly they are mandatory for every person,*" meaning that they are an individual obligation upon every Muslim, contrary to bodily migration which may be mandatory sometimes and not others, or upon some and not others. Likewise is the case with *jihād*: jihād against the self and shayṭān is mandatory at all times, whereas physical *jihād* is a communal obligation at some times. Whoever would like exactitude about the issues pertinent to these two aforementioned migrations should refer to the book *(Ṭarīq) al Hijratayn* by the author [i.e., Ibn al Qayyim (رَحِمَهُ ٱللَّهُ)]. He has brought forth therein what needs no addition.

Muhammad bin Sālih al 'Uthaymīn (رَحِمَهُ ٱللَّهُ) explains:

These lines of poetry are extremely important. They entail sincerity of intention and sincerity in following.

He says: "*Make your heart embark upon two migrations and do not fall asleep. For certainly they are mandatory for every person.*"

His statement, "*make your heart embark upon two migrations*" means make your heart migrate with two migrations. Migration here is to leave off all else while migrating towards them. His statement, "*and do not sleep*" means do not be complacent or lazy, but rather be awake and swift while being ambitious. As for his statement, "*upon every person,*" then does that include the Muslim and the unbeliever, or just the Muslim? The answer is that it includes the Muslim and the unbeliever, because there is no-one who hears the invitation of the Prophet (صَلَّى ٱللَّهُ عَلَيْهِ وَسَلَّمَ) and dies without believing in what he came with except that that person will be from the denizens of

Hellfire. So it is mandatory for every person to migrate with these two migrations.

Sālih al Fawzān (حفظه الله) explains:

Al Hijrah is to abandon something. What is intended here by *al Hijra* is abandonment of falsehood and transitioning to the truth. It constitutes two types: (1.) migrating towards Allah (عَزَّوَجَلَّ) and (2.) migrating to Allah's Messenger (صَلَّى ٱللَّهُ عَلَيْهِ وَسَلَّمَ).

Migrating to Allah (عَزَّوَجَلَّ) is embarked upon by way of sincerity and monotheism. Migrating to Allah's Messenger (صَلَّى ٱللَّهُ عَلَيْهِ وَسَلَّمَ) is embarked upon by way of following and emulating him. This is the migration of the heart. There is also a migration of bodies which is to transfer from the lands of disbelief to the land of Islam.

So there are two migrations: the migration of the heart and the migration of the body. The heart's migration is to go to belief from disbelief, by way of sincerity to Allah (عَزَّوَجَلَّ) and going towards the Messenger (صَلَّى ٱللَّهُ عَلَيْهِ وَسَلَّمَ) through emulation. The bodily migration is done by going away from the lands of disbelief to the lands of the Muslims, fleeing with one's religion. No one is safe except through these two migrations: migrating towards Allah (عَزَّوَجَلَّ) and migrating to the Messenger (صَلَّى ٱللَّهُ عَلَيْهِ وَسَلَّمَ); just as one may not be safe except by migrating from lands of unbelief to the land of Islam.

35. The First Migration: Sincerity

فَالهِجْرَةِ الأُوْلَى إِلَى الرَّحْمَنِ بِالْـ ... إِخْلَاصِ فِي سِرٍّ وَفِي إِعْلَانِ

[35. /(222.)] The first is the migration to al-Raḥmān by way of sincerity inwardly and outwardly (or privately and publicly).

Muhammad bin Sālih al-'Uthaymīn (رَحِمَهُ ٱللَّهُ) explains:

This is the first migration: that you internally make yourself sincere for Allah (عَزَّوَجَلَّ), meaning as pertains what your heart is active in of *khashya* (fear), *tawakkul* (reliance), *raghba* (desire of divine reward), and *rahbah* (dread of divine punishment). As for his statement, "*and outwardly,*" then it means what you do with your bodily limbs of statement and action. It is also possible that what is meant by "*fī sirr*" means what is done privately, while "*wa fī 'ilān*" means (what you do) while people are watching. Both meanings are correct.

36. The Definition of Sincerity

فَالْقَصْدُ وَجْهُ اللهِ بِالْأَقْوَالِ وَالْ ... أَعْمَالِ وَالطَّاعَاتِ وَالشُّكْرَانِ

[36. /(223.)] So the intention is to be for Allah's Face, by words and deeds, acts of obedience and gratitude.

'Abd al-Rahmān al-Sa'dī (رَحِمَهُ ٱللَّهُ) explains:

The definition of sincerity is what he mentioned in the verse of poetry immediately afterwards: *"So the intention is to be for Allah's*

Face, by all words, deeds, acts of obedience, and gratitude." Meaning that the person should not make his intention for anything except Allah's Face.

He should not do so to be seen or heard, or for some selfish worldly reason, such as a person who gives charity, pays the poor-due, or is dutiful to their parents to forego some harm or to multiply wealth by doing so, or hoping that his parents reciprocate with benevolence. Such a person has not intended Allah's Face thereby, so it is upon him to seek Allah's Face first and then he will achieve the aforementioned things secondly.

Muhammad bin Sālih al 'Uthaymīn (رَحِمَهُ ٱللَّهُ) explains:

His saying, "*so the intention is to be for Allah's Face*" means that you are to make your intention for Allah's Face as Allah (تَبَارَكَ وَتَعَالَىٰ) said:

﴿وَاصْبِرْ نَفْسَكَ مَعَ الَّذِينَ يَدْعُونَ رَبَّهُم بِالْغَدَاةِ وَالْعَشِيِّ يُرِيدُونَ وَجْهَهُ ۖ وَلَا تَعْدُ عَيْنَاكَ عَنْهُمْ تُرِيدُ زِينَةَ الْحَيَاةِ الدُّنْيَا ۖ﴾

"And keep yourself patiently with those who call on their Lord morning and afternoon, seeking His Face, and let not your eyes overlook them, desiring the pomp and glitter of the life of the world" [al Kahf: 28]

His statement, "*acts of obedience and gratitude*" is said in the manner of conjoining descriptive attributes onto a particular thing, because all statements and actions are a part of gratitude, and even more than that, gratitude constitutes obedience and enactment of divine commandment.

37. Sincerity Spares a Person from Shirk

فَبِذَاكَ يَنْجُو العَبْدُ مِنْ إِشْرَاكِهِ ... وَيَصِيرُ حَقًّا عَابِدَ الرَّحْمَنِ

[37. /(224.)] By doing that the worshipful-slave is spared from ascribing partners to him, and in doing so becomes a true worshipful-slave for al-Raḥmān.

Muhammad bin Sālih al 'Uthaymīn (رحمه الله) explains:

Meaning that once one makes their intention sincerely for Allah (عَزَّوَجَلَّ) in all of his statements, deeds, acts of obedience, as well as in abandonment of forbidden things, then he is safe from associationism and becomes totally sincere.

38: Migration to the Prophet

والهِجْرَةُ الأُخْرَى إِلَى المَبْعُوثِ بِالْـ ... حَقِّ المُبِينِ وَوَاضِحِ البُرْهَانِ

[38. /(225.)] The other migration is to the one who was dispatched with the unambiguous truth and clear proof.

'Abd al-Rahmān al-Sa'dī (رحمه الله) explains:

The second migration is that which is embarked upon towards the Messenger (صَلَّى ٱللَّهُ عَلَيْهِ وَسَلَّمَ) by way of emulation. The explanation of emulation is what is mentioned in the verse immediate after: *"So he is aligned with the Messenger's statements and actions pertaining what is negated and what is affirmed, without any shiftiness."* Meaning: he appoints that as his judge to which everything else is presented. Whatever conforms to it, he accepts. Whatever differs with it, then he abandons.

Muhammad bin Sālih al 'Uthaymīn (رَحِمَهُ ٱللَّهُ) explains:

His saying, "***the one who was dispatched***" means the Prophet (صَلَّىٰ ٱللَّهُ عَلَيْهِ وَسَلَّمَ). So the second migration is to Allah's Messenger (صَلَّىٰ ٱللَّهُ عَلَيْهِ وَسَلَّمَ) by way of following him and not evading his guidance by way of rushing or delaying, or by way of shifting to the left or to the right. Through this migration you are safe from heterodoxy. So it is mandatory for every Muslim to make his heart embark upon these two migrations.

39. The Reality of The Second Migration

فَيَدُورُ مَعَ قَوْلِ الرَّسُولِ وَفِعْلِهِ ... نَفْيًا وَإِثْبَاتًا بِلَا رَوَغَانِ

[39. /(226.)] So he is centered upon the Messenger's statements and actions pertaining what is negated and what is affirmed, without any shiftiness.

Muhammad bin Sālih al 'Uthaymīn (رَحِمَهُ ٱللَّهُ) explains:

Meaning that he is aligned with the Messenger's statements and actions. "*pertaining negation*" — whenever the Messenger (صَلَّىٰ ٱللَّهُ عَلَيْهِ وَسَلَّمَ) negated a thing, and "*affirmation*" whenever he affirmed a thing. As for his statement, "*without any shiftiness*," then "*rawaghān*" [i.e., shiftiness, slyness] is the act not going straight in one's trajectory, as is done by foxes. The fox is clever, it swerves when it sees its enemy, regardless of whether that be a person or an animal. It senses him and runs, shifting to the left and to the right, or even backtracking, making its pursuer pass him by multiple steps at which point how could they backtrack?

The person is obligated to align himself with the Messenger's statements and actions, negating what he negated and affirming what he affirmed. In the matter of affirming information (from the Prophet صَلَّى ٱللَّهُ عَلَيْهِ وَسَلَّمَ), he unhesitatingly believes. He does not inquire as to how, what, and why? In the matter of commandment, he obeys and does not hesitate. He does not inquire as to whether this commandment is mandatory or voluntary. As pertains negating of information, then he is certain about negating anything that the Messenger (صَلَّى ٱللَّهُ عَلَيْهِ وَسَلَّمَ) negated while being certain when affirming whatever he affirmed. In the matter of prohibition, he abandons what he prohibited without inquiring as to whether or not this prohibition is indicative of dislike or prohibition. So when the Messenger (صَلَّى ٱللَّهُ عَلَيْهِ وَسَلَّمَ) prohibits him from something, he must say: we hear and obey. Then he abstains. When he is ordered to do something, he must say: we hear and obey. Then he must do it.

Accordingly, I do not recall any of the *Ṣaḥāba*, when ordered by the Prophet (صَلَّى ٱللَّهُ عَلَيْهِ وَسَلَّمَ) to do something, saying: O Allah's Messenger! Is this mandatory or recommended? Yes, in the matter of personal opinion, they would say that, as is mentioned about al Ḥubāb bin al Mundhir (رَضِيَ ٱللَّهُ عَنْهُ) that when the Prophet (صَلَّى ٱللَّهُ عَلَيْهِ وَسَلَّمَ) encamped at the bottom of the wells of Badr, he said: "O Allah's Messenger! Look at this encampment: is it a location that Allah (عَزَّ وَجَلَّ) instructed you to choose, so that we should not move beyond it or before it? Or is (chosen) out of opinion, war-fighting, and strategy?" He (صَلَّى ٱللَّهُ عَلَيْهِ وَسَلَّمَ) said: "Rather, it is out of opinion, war-fighting, and strategy." So he said: "This is not the (best) place. Rather, we should move forward to the last well, so that the disbelievers cannot enter upon us." As for whether he ever told them to do something to which they responded: O Allah's Messenger is it mandatory, permitted, or recommended? Then, the answer to this is that they did not speak like this. May Allah be pleased with them. So when they were invited to Allah (عَزَّ وَجَلَّ) and His Messenger (صَلَّى ٱللَّهُ عَلَيْهِ وَسَلَّمَ) they said: We hear and we obey.

VII. Restricting Arbitration to Two Judges
Synopsis of Lines 40-46:

40. Men's Statements are to be Weighed Against the Revelation

41. & 42. The Revelation is the Source of All Justice, & it is the Cure & Guide

43. The Sunnah is the Second Arbiter

44. The Reality of Everything Besides These Two Judges

45. & 46. No Honor or Cooperation with the People of Falsehood

VII. Restricting Arbitration to Two Judges (Lines 40-46)

وَيُحَكِّمُ الوَحْيَ المُبِينَ عَلَى الَّذي ... قَالَ الشُّيوُخُ فَعِنْدَهُ حَكَمَانِ

[40. /(227.)] He arbitrates with the unambiguous revelation over what was said by Shuyūkh. Therefore, he only has two matters by which to judge.

لاَ يَحْكُمَانِ بِبَاطِلٍ أَبَداً وَكُلُّ ... العَدْلِ قَدْ جَاءَتْ بِهِ الحَكَمَانِ

[41. /(228.)] Neither of them ever judge in falsehood, rather every justice has been brought by these two judges.

وَهُمَا كِتَابُ اللهِ أَعْدَلُ حَاكِمٍ ... فِيهِ الشِّفَا وَهِدَايَةُ الحَيْرَانِ

[42. /(229.)] These are: Allah's book, which is the fairest arbiter, entailing the cure and guidance for the bewildered.

والحَاكِمِ الثَّانِي كَلَامُ رَسُولِهِ ... مَا ثَمَّ غَيْرُهُمَا لِذِي إِيْمَانِ

[43. /(230.)] And the second judge is the Messenger's speech. There is none other besides these two for the person of faith.

فَإِذَا دَعَوْكَ لِغَيْرِ حُكْمِهِمَا فَلَا ... سَمْعًا لِدَاعِي الْكُفْرِ وَالعِصْيَانِ

[44. /(231.)] If they invite you to anything other than the judgement of these two, then do not listen to one inviting to disbelief and disobedience.

قُلْ لَا كَرَامَةَ لا، ولا نُعْمَى وَلَا ... طَوْعاً لِمَنْ يَدْعُو إِلَى طُغْيَانِ

[45. /(232.)] Say: no honor, no satisfaction and no cooperation for one inviting to transgression.

وَإِذَا دُعِيتَ إِلَى الرَّسُولِ فَقُلْ لَهُمْ ... سَمْعًا وَطَوْعًا لَسْتُ ذَا عِصْيَانِ

[46. /(233.)] If you are invited to the Messenger, then say to them: I hear and obey, and I am not from the disobedient.

Synopsis of Lines 40-46

Muhammad Khalīl Harrās (رَحِمَهُ ٱللَّهُ) summarizes:

In these lines of poetry, the author alludes to a tremendous fundamental from which most people have strayed, resultantly falling into differing and dissent between themselves. They miss out on the truth according to their degree of neglecting it. Namely, that is employing the clear revelation for arbitration in all issues of religion — in its foundations and secondary tenets — and preferring it over blind-following *Mashā'ikh* and ancestors in their evidence-void statements. So there are two judges that judge exclusively by way of all that is true and fair. It is unfathomable that anything else would emanate from the two. So the first is Allah's Book which no falsehood can approach from in front of it or behind it. Whoever speaks with it speaks truthfully and whoever judges by it has exacted justice. It entails the cure from all diseases of the heart and the guidance for every astray and bewildered person.

The second is the speech of Allah's Messenger (صَلَّى ٱللَّهُ عَلَيْهِ وَسَلَّمَ) — who Allah (عَزَّ وَجَلَّ) commanded to judge between people using that which He revealed to him. He was to convey it them with clear conveyance, elucidating for them what had been sent down to them. He (تَبَارَكَ وَتَعَالَىٰ) said:

﴿ فَلَا وَرَبِّكَ لَا يُؤْمِنُونَ حَتَّىٰ يُحَكِّمُوكَ فِيمَا شَجَرَ بَيْنَهُمْ ثُمَّ لَا يَجِدُوا فِي أَنفُسِهِمْ حَرَجًا مِّمَّا قَضَيْتَ وَيُسَلِّمُوا تَسْلِيمًا ﴾

"But no, by your Lord, they will not [truly] believe until they make you, [O Muhammad (ﷺ)], judge concerning that over which they dispute among themselves and then find within themselves no discomfort from what you have judged and submit in [full, willing] submission." [al-Nisā': 65].

Therefore, when a person is invited to anything besides the judgement of these two, then it is compulsory to reject that with every sort of refusal and not to comply with anyone inviting him thereto. He is to say "no" with the fullness of his mouth: no honor, no thank you, and no obedience to those who invite to unbelief and transgression. However, if he is invited Allah and His Messenger, then he is to focus on hearing and obeying without refusal or haughtiness. He said:

﴿ إِنَّمَا كَانَ قَوْلَ الْمُؤْمِنِينَ إِذَا دُعُوا إِلَى اللَّهِ وَرَسُولِهِ لِيَحْكُمَ بَيْنَهُمْ أَن يَقُولُوا سَمِعْنَا وَأَطَعْنَا ﴾

"The only statement of the [true] believers when they are called to Allah and His Messenger to judge between them is that they say, 'We hear and we obey.'" [al-Nūr: 51].

40. All Statements must be Weighed Against the Revelation

وَيُحَكِّمُ الوَحْيَ المُبِينَ عَلَى الَّذِي ... قَالَ الشُّيُوخُ فَعِنْدَهُ حَكَمَانِ

[40. /(227.)] He arbitrates with the unambiguous revelation over what was said by Shuyūkh. Therefore, he only has two matters by which to judge.

Muhammad bin Sālih al 'Uthaymīn (رَحِمَهُ ٱللَّهُ) *explains:*

His statement, "*the unambiguous revelation*" means the Book and the Sunnah. His statement, "what was said by the Shuyūkh, means the *fuqahā'* — the scholars of a school of *fiqh* for example, or the scholars of *kalām* (speculative theology) who are followed. Most of those who are fanatical for schools of jurisprudence are as such that if you said that something is impermissible, they they would retort that it is permissible. So when you say: where is the proof? They say it is in the book of so-and-so. The reality is that the speech of the people of knowledge requires proof and is not employed as a proof. It is not an evidence, but rather the proof is entailed in that which Allah (عَزَّوَجَلَّ) and the Messenger (صَلَّىٱللَّهُعَلَيْهِوَسَلَّمَ) said. So he says, "*He arbitrates with the unambiguous revelation over what was said by Shuyūkh.*" Then he says: "*therefore, he only has two matters by which to judge,*" namely, these are the Book and the *Sunnah*, due to Allah's statement (تَبَارَكَوَتَعَالَىٰ):

﴿ فَإِن تَنَازَعْتُمْ فِي شَيْءٍ فَرُدُّوهُ إِلَى اللَّهِ وَالرَّسُولِ إِن كُنتُمْ تُؤْمِنُونَ بِاللَّهِ وَالْيَوْمِ الْآخِرِ ۚ ذَٰلِكَ خَيْرٌ وَأَحْسَنُ تَأْوِيلًا ﴾

"And if you disagree over anything, refer it to Allah and the Messenger, if you should believe in Allah and the Last Day. That is the best [way] and best in result." [al-Nisā': 59].

Also, He (تَبَارَكَوَتَعَالَىٰ) said:

﴿ فَلَا وَرَبِّكَ لَا يُؤْمِنُونَ حَتَّىٰ يُحَكِّمُوكَ فِيمَا شَجَرَ بَيْنَهُمْ ثُمَّ لَا يَجِدُوا فِي أَنفُسِهِمْ حَرَجًا مِّمَّا قَضَيْتَ وَيُسَلِّمُوا تَسْلِيمًا ﴾

"But no, by your Lord, they will not [truly] believe until they make you, [O Muhammad (صَلَّى ٱللَّهُ عَلَيْهِ وَسَلَّمَ)], judge concerning that over which they dispute among themselves and then find within themselves no discomfort from what you have judged and submit in [full, willing] submission." [al-Nisā': 65].

Sālih al Fawzān (حفظه الله) explains:

One is to use the Book and the Sunnah to judge the statements of shuyūkh through analyzing their statements in accordance to the Book and the Sunnah, no matter how great their status. Whatever conforms to the Book and Sunnah is accepted. Whatever opposes them is rejected, even if it be from the greatest of *Shaykhs*. The Qurān and Sunnah is above everyone.

41. & 42. The Revelation is the Source of All Justice, & it is the Cure & Guide

لاَ يُحْكُمَانِ بِبَاطِلٍ أَبَداً وَكُلُّ ... العَدْلِ قَدْ جَاءَتْ بِهِ الحَكَمَانِ

[41. /(228.)] Neither of them ever judge in falsehood, rather every justice has been brought by these two judges.

وَهُمَا كِتَابُ اللهِ أَعْدَلُ حَاكِمٍ ... فِيهِ الشِّفَا وَهِدَايَةُ الحَيْرَانِ

[42. /(229.)] These are: Allah's book, which is the fairest arbiter, entailing the cure and guidance for the bewildered.

'Abd al-Rahmān al-Sa'dī (رَحِمَهُ ٱللَّهُ) explains:

Meaning: pertaining all events and everything people need, then the Quran contains what completely explains and elucidates it, as the author mentioned in *'Ilām al Muwaqi'īn*.[17]

Muhammad bin Sālih al 'Uthaymīn (رَحِمَهُ ٱللَّهُ) explains:

He said the truth. The *Qurān* and Sunnah cannot come with any falsehood. What is meant by the Sunnah is whatever is authentic from the Prophet (صَلَّىٰ ٱللَّهُ عَلَيْهِ وَسَلَّمَ). No doubt the fairest book is Allah's Book. If all of creation were to unite to produce something comparable to the Qurān they could not produce its likes, because it consists of the fairest judgement.

As for his statement, "*entailing the cure*," then curing means recovery from illness. But which type of cure is in the Qurān? Is it the physical cure or the spiritual cure? The answer is that it is both of them. Allah (تَبَارَكَ وَتَعَالَىٰ) said:

﴿يَا أَيُّهَا النَّاسُ قَدْ جَاءَتْكُم مَّوْعِظَةٌ مِّن رَّبِّكُمْ وَشِفَاءٌ لِّمَا فِي الصُّدُورِ وَهُدًى وَرَحْمَةٌ لِّلْمُؤْمِنِينَ﴾

"O mankind, there has to come to you instruction from your Lord and healing for what is in the breasts and guidance and mercy for the believers." [Yunus: 57]

---

17 (1/263)

This is the spiritual cure. Also, the Prophet (صَلَّى ٱللَّهُ عَلَيْهِ وَسَلَّمَ) said to a person who recited the *Fātiḥa* over a person bitten by a scorpion, who then stood up with rigor as though released from being tied down — he said to the reciter:

وَمَا يُدْرِيكَ أَنَّهَا رُقْيَةٌ؟

"How did you know that it is *Ruqya*?"[18]

So the cure that the Quran procures and entails is of the two types: physical and spiritual.

As for his statement, "*and guidance for the bewildered*," then yes, by Allah! It is guidance for the bewildered, meaning the person who is confused, hesitant, and doubtful. Such a person will find guidance in the *Qurān*. He will find in the *Qurān* the enjoyment and tranquility of the heart, the opening of the chest, and the relief of his soul.

No matter how much you request doctors to alleviate what is in your heart, then you will never find anything comparable to the the *Qurān*. But who will this transpire for? The answer is that it is only for those who believe, as Allah (تَبَارَكَ وَتَعَالَىٰ) said:

﴿ قُلْ هُوَ لِلَّذِينَ آمَنُوا هُدًى وَشِفَاءٌ ﴾

"Say, 'It is, for those who believe, a guidance and cure.'" [Fuṣṣilat: 44].

Someone who is not a believer is not going to benefit from it. Read Allah's statement (تَبَارَكَ وَتَعَالَىٰ):

---

[18] Collected by al Bukhārī (2156) and Muslim (2201)

﴿ وَإِذَا مَا أُنزِلَتْ سُورَةٌ فَمِنْهُم مَّن يَقُولُ أَيُّكُمْ زَادَتْهُ هَٰذِهِ إِيمَانًا ﴾

"And whenever a surah is revealed, there are among the hypocrites those who say, 'Which of you has this increased faith?'"[al-Tawbah: 124].

Then Allah (تَبَارَكَ وَتَعَالَىٰ) went on to say:

﴿ فَأَمَّا الَّذِينَ آمَنُوا فَزَادَتْهُمْ إِيمَانًا وَهُمْ يَسْتَبْشِرُونَ (124) وَأَمَّا الَّذِينَ فِي قُلُوبِهِم مَّرَضٌ فَزَادَتْهُمْ رِجْسًا إِلَىٰ رِجْسِهِمْ وَمَاتُوا وَهُمْ كَافِرُونَ ﴾

"As for those who believed, it has increased them in faith, while they are rejoicing. But as for those in whose hearts is disease, it has [only] increased them in evil [in addition] to their evil. And they will have died while they are disbelievers." [al-Tawbah: 124-125]

Someone other than a believer will never see the *Qurān* as the cure and will not benefit from the *Qurān*, rather:

﴿ إِذَا تُتْلَىٰ عَلَيْهِ آيَاتُنَا قَالَ أَسَاطِيرُ الْأَوَّلِينَ ﴾

"When Our verses are recited to him, he says, 'Legends of the ancients.'" [al Muṭaffifīn: 13].

This is because he does not benefit from it. "*The legends of the ancients*" is like when we say ancient myths, because they do not benefit (that person). The stronger a person's faith in Allah (عَزَّوَجَلَّ) is, the more the *Qurān* will benefit him in curing the sickness of the heart, enlightening the heart, expanding the chest, and bringing tranquility to the heart. Try it and find out for yourself.

It is amazing that personally I sometimes search for the ruling on a particular issue in what I possess of the books of the *Fuqahā'* and in that which I know of the Sunnah, yet do not find it. Then I reflect over a verse in the *Qurān* that alludes to the ruling of that issue. So when I further reflect, I find that the ruling was in the *Qurān*. So the person finds peace at the fact that the *Qurān* is:

﴿ تِبْيَانًا لِّكُلِّ شَيْءٍ ﴾

"An exposition of all things" [al-Naḥl: 98].

And it is the guidance for every bewildered person.

43. The Sunnah is the Second Arbiter

والحَاكِم الثَّاني كَلَامُ رَسُولِهِ ... مَا ثَمَّ غَيْرُهُمَا لِذِي إِيْمَانِ

[43. /(230.)] And the second judge is the Messenger's speech. There is none other besides these two for the person of faith.

Muhammad bin Sālih al 'Uthaymīn (رحمه الله) explains:

As for his statement, "*and the second judge is the Messenger's speech*," then the author qualified it with a restrictive clause, saying "*for the person of faith*." The Messenger's speech, as well as his practice, is the second judge. You have read Allah's statement (تبارك وتعالى):

﴿ فَلَا وَرَبِّكَ لَا يُؤْمِنُونَ حَتَّىٰ يُحَكِّمُوكَ فِيمَا شَجَرَ بَيْنَهُمْ ﴾

"But no, by your Lord, they will not [truly] believe until they make you, [O Muhammad (صلى الله عليه وسلم)], judge concerning that over which they dispute among themselves." [al-Nisā': 65].

Meaning: as pertains what happens between you of differing.

﴿ ثُمَّ لَا يَجِدُوا فِي أَنفُسِهِمْ حَرَجًا مِّمَّا قَضَيْتَ وَيُسَلِّمُوا تَسْلِيمًا ﴾

"...and then find within themselves no discomfort from what you have judged and submit in [full, willing] submission."[al-Nisā': 65]

44. The Reality of Everything Besides These Two

فَإِذَا دَعَوْكَ لِغَيْرِ حُكْمِهِمَا فَلَا ... سَمْعًا لِدَاعِي الْكُفْرِ وَالعِصْيَانِ

[44. /(231.)] If they invite you to anything other than the judgement of these two, then do not listen to one inviting to disbelief and disobedience.

Muhammad bin Sālih al 'Uthaymīn (رَحِمَهُ ٱللَّهُ) explains:

The author provides us with the benefit that whoever judges by other than what was brought in the Book and *Sunnah*, then his situation is between two matters: either he is a disbeliever, or either he is disobedient. As such he said, "*then do not listen to one inviting to disbelief and disobedience*."

Sālih al Fawzān (حفظه الله) explains:

When they invite to the principles of human reasoning, speculative theology and man-made laws, then say: I do not listen, nor do I obey; rather come to the Book and the Sunnah, not to the principles of so-and-so, or dialectics, speculative theology and what they call logical proofs. All of this is multi-faceted falsehood. We use the Book and the Sunnah for reference.

﴿فَإِمَّا يَأْتِيَنَّكُم مِّنِّي هُدًى فَمَنِ اتَّبَعَ هُدَايَ فَلَا يَضِلُّ وَلَا يَشْقَىٰ﴾

"And if there should come to you guidance from Me - then whoever follows My guidance will neither go astray [in the world] nor suffer [in the Hereafter]." [Ṭaha: 123].

This is the path of salvation.

45. & 46. No Honor or Cooperation with the People of Falsehood

قُلْ لَا كَرَامَةَ لَا، وَلَا نُعْمَى وَلَا ... طَوْعاً لِمَنْ يَدْعُو إِلَى طُغْيَانِ

[45. /(232.)] Say: no honor, no satisfaction and no cooperation with anyone inviting to tyranny.

وَإِذَا دُعِيتَ إِلَى الرَّسُولِ فَقُلْ لَهُمْ ... سَمْعًا وَطَوْعًا لَسْتُ ذَا عِصْيَانِ

[46. /(233.)] If you are invited to the Messenger, then say to them: I hear and obey, and I am not from the disobedient.

Muhammad bin Sālih al 'Uthaymīn (رحمه الله) explains:

This is what is mandatory upon the Muslim to say (inwardly) with his heart and verbally: I do not hear or obey those who invite to transgression. But how is that person inviting to transgression? We say: that is because any person inviting to a law other than that of Allah and His Messenger is a tyrant, as Allah (تَبَارَكَ وَتَعَالَى) said:

﴿أَلَمْ تَرَ إِلَى الَّذِينَ يَزْعُمُونَ أَنَّهُمْ آمَنُوا بِمَا أُنزِلَ إِلَيْكَ وَمَا أُنزِلَ مِن قَبْلِكَ يُرِيدُونَ أَن يَتَحَاكَمُوا إِلَى الطَّاغُوتِ وَقَدْ أُمِرُوا أَن يَكْفُرُوا بِهِ وَيُرِيدُ الشَّيْطَانُ أَن يُضِلَّهُمْ ضَلَالًا بَعِيدًا وَإِذَا قِيلَ لَهُمْ تَعَالَوْا إِلَى مَا أَنزَلَ اللَّهُ وَإِلَى الرَّسُولِ رَأَيْتَ الْمُنَافِقِينَ يَصُدُّونَ عَنكَ صُدُودًا﴾

"Have you not seen those who claim to have believed in what was revealed to you, [O Muhammad (صَلَّى اللَّهُ عَلَيْهِ وَسَلَّمَ)], and what was revealed before you? They wish to refer legislation to Taghut, while they were commanded to reject it; and Satan wishes to lead them far astray. And when it is said to them, 'Come to what Allah has revealed and to the Messenger,' you see the hypocrites turning away from you in aversion." [al-Nisā': 60-61]

So the author's statement, "*inviting to tyranny*" is in agreement with the aforementioned verse.

Therefore, whatever opposes Allah's law is tyranny, and whoever invites to that is a *ṭāghūt*. So do you want to be from the people of faith or the people of *ṭāghūt*? Then answer is: from the people of faith.

Sālih al Fawzān (حفظه الله) explains:

This is just as (Allah) (تَبَارَكَ وَتَعَالَى) said:

﴿إِنَّمَا كَانَ قَوْلَ الْمُؤْمِنِينَ إِذَا دُعُوا إِلَى اللَّهِ وَرَسُولِهِ لِيَحْكُمَ بَيْنَهُمْ أَن يَقُولُوا سَمِعْنَا وَأَطَعْنَا﴾

"The only statement of the [true] believers when they are called to Allah and His Messenger to judge between them is that they say, 'We hear and we obey.'" [al-Nūr: 51].

VIII. The True Cause of Victory

Synopsis of Lines 47-51:

47. & 48. The Futility of the Opposition

49. Righteous Deeds:
The Best Means for Victory

50. Victory is Not by Numerical Superiority

51. How the Ṣaḥāba Conquered the Hearts

VIII. The True Cause of Victory

وَإِذَا تَكَاثَرَتْ الخُصُومُ وَصَيَّحُوا ... فَاثْبُتْ فَصَيْحَتُهُمْ كَمِثْلِ دُخَانِ

[47. /(234.)] When the opponents become many and the scream in commotion, then be firm, for their screaming is like nothing but smoke.

يَرْقَى إِلَى الأَوْجِ الْرَّفِيعِ وَبَعْدَهُ ... يَهْوِي إِلَى قَعْرِ الحَضِيضِ الدَّانِي

[48. /(235.)] It rises up to a high point, after which it blows away to the nearest low surface.

هَذَا وَإِنَّ قِتَالَ حِزْبِ اللهِ بِالْـ ... أَعْمَالِ لاَ بِكَتَائِبِ الشُّجْعَانِ

[49. /(236.)] Additionally, the fighting of Allah's faction is by way of deeds, not by contingents of brave warriors.

وَاللهِ مَا فَتَحُوا البِلَادَ بِكَثْرَةٍ ... أَنَّى وَأَعْدَاءُهُمْ بِلَا حُسْبَانِ

[50. /(237.)] By Allah they did not conquer the land by way of numbers! How could that be when their enemies were unimaginable?

وَكَذَاكَ مَا فَتَحُوا القُلُوبَ بِهَذِهِ الْـ ... آرَاءِ بَلْ بِالْعِلْمِ وَالإِيْمَانِ

[51. /(238.)] Likewise, they did not conquer the hearts by means of these opinions, but rather it was by knowledge and faith.

Synopsis of Lines 47-51

Muhammad Khalīl Harrās (رحمه الله) summarizes:

It is compulsory that the proponent of truth who is holding fast to the revealed religion be apathetic to the multitude of opponents and that he not be scared by their screaming and clamoring. For indeed, the plot of falsehood is weak. It eventually fades into oblivion, rapidly disappearing, just as smoke rises to the upper part of the sky, only to thereafter decline to the lowest surface.

As for the people of truth, then they do not fight their foes by numerical might but rather, they do so by way of their noble deeds and righteous character. Had the issue been a numerical one, then they would never have been able to conquer the ancient dynasties or to face down those formidable armies who had had surpassed them tens, or rather hundreds, of times beyond their numbers.

Similarly, they would not have conquered peoples' hearts for guidance nor would they have endeared Islam to them through the likes of the innovated opinions touted by the feigners of philosophy and the speculative theologians. Their propagation was substantiated solely upon knowledge and faith which united the hearts around them and convinced those people to be cooperative and accommodating.

47. & 48. The Futility of the Opposition

وَإِذَا تَكَاثَرَتْ الخُصُومُ وَصَيَّحُوا ... فَاثْبُتْ فَصَيْحَتُهُمْ كَمِثْلِ دُخَانِ

[47. /(234.)] When the opponents become many and they scream in commotion, then be firm, for their screaming is like nothing but smoke.

يَرْقَى إِلَى الأَوْجِ الرَّفِيعِ وَبَعْدَهُ ... يَهْوِي إِلَى قَعْرِ الحَضِيضِ الدَّانِي

[48. /(235.)] It rises up to a high point, after which it blows away to the nearest low surface.

'Abd al-Rahmān al-Sa'dī (رحمه الله) explains:

It rises up to *al awj,* meaning to a high, lofty point. Its opposite is *al ḥaḍīḍ,* which is the low, sunken part of the land.

Sālih al Fawzān (حفظه الله) explains:

The yelling of the people of *bida'* is like vanishing smoke. Smoke becomes dense and obstructs the sky, rising up high. Then it quickly drops down and vanishes. That is similar to the situation of falsehood.

Muhammad bin Sālih al 'Uthaymīn (رحمه الله) explains:

His statement, "*when the opponents become many,*" means that when you are alone in your land inviting to the Sunnah and to following the Salaf while there are a lot of enemies inviting to their false school of thought, then it is mandatory upon you not to behave defeatedly, because if your behave defeatedly, then you have caused defeat of the truth. Instead, be firm.

How frightened your enemies will become when they see that you are firm! As for his statement, "*for their yelling is like nothing but smoke*," then he has likened them to smoke. Their voices, clamoring, words, and propaganda rises high above, yet if a person stands firm, then the smoke will soon break up and disperse to the right and left, doing the person no harm. If it rises up to the atmosphere, then eventually it will come back down and fall low. This is one of the most amazing and precise comparisons.

Secondly, when they rise up against you, then falsehood will ultimately fall low and descend. This is because smoke ascends and then descends quickly due to the winds shoving it back to the ground. As for his statement, "*smoke that rises up to a high point*," then the author has explained the similitude only as relates to (falsehood) rising high. However, we have added to that its lack of staying-power for one who stands firm. In such a case it undoubtedly breaks up and dissipates.

49. Righteous Deeds: The Best Means of Victory

هَذَا وَإِنَّ قِتَالَ حِزْبِ اللهِ بِالْـ... أَعْمَالِ لاَ بِكَتَائِبِ الشُّجْعَانِ

[49. /(236.)] Additionally, the fighting of Allah's faction is by way of deeds, not by contingents of brave warriors.

Ahmad bin 'Isā al-Najdī (رَحِمَهُ ٱللَّهُ) explains:

Meaning that in the beginning, Islam was strange as (the Prophet) (صَلَّىٱللَّهُعَلَيْهِوَسَلَّمَ) said: "***Islam began as something strange and will return to being something strange just as it began.***" Likewise, there has come in the ḥadīth of 'Amr b. 'Abasa when he came to the Prophet (صَلَّىٱللَّهُعَلَيْهِوَسَلَّمَ) prior to him publicly proclaiming (the message) in Makkah. He said to him: "Who is with you in this matter?" He said: "One freeman and one slave." Meaning Abu Bakr and Bilāl. Then Allah (عَزَّوَجَلَّ) granted victory to he and his companions, as is well-known from the books of *Sīrah*.

Also, ***katā'ib*** is the plural form of ***katība***, which is a battalion of horsemen and soldiers.

'Abd al-Rahmān al-Sa'dī (رَحِمَهُ ٱللَّهُ) explains:

Meaning: Islam began as something strange and what they achieved of victory and conquests were not because of their great numbers or equipment. It was entirely because of something that had settled in their hearts and was proven by their actions.

Sālih al Fawzān (حفظه الله) explains:

Allah's faction fights by way of belief and righteous deeds, not by way of a sizable army. Rather, righteous deeds are simply their sole weapon.

Muhammad bin Sālih al 'Uthaymīn (رحمه الله) explains:

As for his statement, "***not by contingents of brave warriors,***" then it means not by contingents of brave warriors alone. Otherwise, it is known that the faction of Allah combat their enemies with deeds and likewise with battalions.[19] Were it not for the battalions and the banners of *jihād*, then victory over Allah's enemies would not transpire. So Allah's enemies are fought by way of two matters: the first is deeds and the second is battalions of brave soldiers.

He spoke the truth. Righteous deeds, virtuous character, and good dealings conquer the enemy's heart more than do swords. As such, we find in the study of history that many disbelieving rulers accepted Islam without any fighting once it was explained to them. When they were told how the Muslims were, they accepted Islam. When Heraclius was told of the Messenger's qualities, he admitted that he was the truth, however — and Allah's refuge is sought — his greed for rulership prevented him from becoming Muslim.

50. Victory is Not by Numerical Superiority

وَاللهِ مَا فَتَحُوا البِلَادَ بِكَثْرَةٍ ... أَنَّى وَأَعْدَاءُهُمْ بِلَا حُسْبَانِ

[50. /(237.)] By Allah they did not conquer the land by way of numbers! How could that be when their enemies were unimaginable?

---

[19] T.N. According to the wise laws and humane ethics governing such matters in Islamic jurisprudence, which is a vast topic far beyond the general scope of this book.

Muhammad bin Sālih al 'Uthaymīn (رَحِمَهُ ٱللَّهُ) explains:

As for his statement, "*by Allah! They did not conquer the land by way of numbers,*" then he is alluding to the *Ṣaḥāba* (رَضِيَ ٱللَّهُ عَنْهُمْ) and the *Salaf* of this Ummah. So they did not conquer the land by numerical strength. "*How could that be when their enemies were unimaginable?*" This is true and it entails a refutation of those who say that the Muslims conquered the lands with weapons and war. This is the statement of Islām's enemies. This is because if they purport that, then that infers that the Muslims were tyrannical oppressors who conquered the land with the power of weaponry. This is not said by anyone except our enemies from the orientalists and their peons. The lands were conquered by doing righteous deeds and the hearts were conquered by way of knowledge.

As for doing righteous deeds, then during the era of the *Ṣaḥāba* (رَضِيَ ٱللَّهُ عَنْهُمْ), when the disbelievers saw the enslavement and subjugation that their tyrants and rulers subjected them to, while seeing what the *Ṣaḥāba* (رَضِيَ ٱللَّهُ عَنْهُمْ) were practicing and how their highest chief and ruler would be in their midst with a patched garment — sleeping on a mound of dirt in the masjid without any guard, while both the young and old were able to speak to him, and how he would address the people and a woman could respond to him and these sorts of things — do souls who retain their original nature accept or reject these sorts of people? The answer is that they accept them, by Allah! So their hearts became conquered before their lands were conquered.

So by way of these noble actions and virtuous characteristics they conquered the lands and not because of numerical or material strength. Were we to contrast between them and their enemies pertaining numerical and material strength, then which of the two would have had more of these? The answer is their enemies innumerably outnumbered them many times over. The same is the case with materiel. Yet, they conquered the land with these deeds.

Sālih al Fawzān (حفظه الله) explains:

The Muslims did not conquer the East and the West by having large armies, because their adversaries from Persia and Byzantium were more numerous than them. Rather, they only conquered it by way of faith and correct belief. Also, they did not conquer the hearts through speculative theology, and a lot of talking and opinions. Instead, they conquered them with the Book and the Sunnah.

So they impacted the hearts, which were then filled with knowledge and faith — with the Book and the Sunnah — not with the doctrine of this one or that one. They were victorious entirely because of sound creed and beneficial knowledge. So they disseminated knowledge in the East and the West, and multitudes of people entered into Allah's religion. The Muslim empire spread by way of these two means: true *jihād*, equipped with the material means, and by way of beneficial knowledge.

51. How the *Ṣaḥāba* Conquered the Hearts

وَكَذَاكَ مَا فَتَحُوا القُلُوبَ بِهَذِهِ الـ... آرَاءِ بَلْ بِالْعِلْمِ وَالإِيْمَانِ

[51. /(238.)] Likewise, they did not conquer the hearts by means of these opinions, but rather it was by knowledge and faith.

'Abd al-Raḥmān al-Sa'dī (رحمه الله) explains:

The shut heart does not recognize good, and even if it does recognize it, it is not elevated by it. Opening it occurs through beneficial knowledge and righteous action, not by the opinions of innovators, pretentious *Jahmites* and others.

Muḥammad bin Ṣāliḥ al 'Uthaymīn (رحمه الله) explains:

He is saying that likewise, they conquered the hearts by way of knowledge and faith, not by the principles of Greek logic. He spoke the truth. If the Muslim creed was presented to their enemies in the manner that the speculative theologians present it, would they believe? They would never believe, but rather that would only serve to increase their aversion. Yet the Muslim's creed is easy and simple. The bedouin comes and says that I testify that there is nothing deserving of worship as a deity except for Allah and I testify that Muḥammad is Allah's Messenger (صَلَّى ٱللَّهُ عَلَيْهِ وَسَلَّمَ), and then he goes along his way. He learns the creed from these two statements.

IX. The Reality of Courage
Synopsis of Lines 52-58:

52. The First Type of Courage

53. The Second Type of Courage

54. What Happens When These Two Combine?

55. Selecting Well-Matched Opponents

56. - 58. Experienced Advice About People

IX. The Reality of Courage (Lines 52-58)

وَشَجَاعَةُ الفُرْسَانِ نَفْسُ الزُّهْدِ فِي ... نَفْسٍ، وَذَا مَحْذُورُ كُلِّ جَبَانِ

[52. /(239.)] The warrior's courage is precisely zuhd (abstemiousness) pertaining one's life, whereas that is something from which every coward is deprived.

وَشَجَاعَةُ الحُكَّامِ وَالْعُلَمَاءِ زُهْـ ... ـدٌ فِي الثَّنَا مِنْ كُلِّ ذِي بُطْلَانِ

[53. /(240.)] The courage of the rulers and the scholars is disinterest in being praised by every person of falsehood.

فَإِذَا هُمَا اجْتَمَعَا لِقَلْبِ صَادِقٍ ... شَدَّتْ رَكَائِبُهُ إِلَى الرَّحْمَنِ

[54. /(241.)] When these two unite[20] within the heart of a person of genuineness, then his steeds will gallop quickly to al-Raḥmān.

وَاقْصِدْ إِلَى الأَقْرَانِ لاَ أَطْرَافِهَا ... فَالْعِزُّ تَحْتَ مَقَاتِلِ الأَقْرَانِ

[55. /(242.)] Seek out the most worthy opponents and not the outer flanks. Honor is found within the contending with worthy opponents.

وَاسْمَعْ نَصِيحَةَ مَنْ لَهُ خُبْرٌ بِمَا ... عِنْدَ الوَرَى مِنْ كَثْرَةِ الجَوَلَانِ

[56. /(243.)] Listen to the advice of one well-informed of what the people possess due to abundant encounters.

---

[20] meaning: (1.) *zuhd* regarding one's life and (2.) *zuhd* regarding people's praise.

مَا عِنْدَهُمْ وَاللهِ خَيْرٌ غَيْرَ مَا ... أَخَذُوهُ عَمَّنْ جَاءَ بِالْقُرَآنِ

[57. /(244.)] By Allah! They have no good with them save that which they received from the one who came with the Qurān.

والكُلُّ بَعْدُ فَبِدْعَةٌ أَوْ فِرْيَةٌ ... أَوْ بَحْثُ تَشْكِيكٍ وَرَأْيُ فُلَانِ

[58. /(245.)] Everything else thereafter is innovation, fabrication or skeptical research and the opinion of fulān [i.e., so-and-so].

Synopsis of Lines 52-58

Muhammad Khalīl Harrās (رحمه الله) summarizes:

The author categorizes courage into:

(1.) Physical courage, which the cavalry implements on the battlefield. He defines it as disinterest in living and deeming life to be of little worth during the clamor of combat. The coward is unable to do this and defiantly avoids it.

(2.) Spiritual courage, which is incorporated by the scholars and rulers who speak the truth without fearing anyone in doing so.

He defines it being disinterested in the praise and commendation that the people of falsehood issue to those who allow them to persist in their falsehood without confronting them with the truth, fearing their commotion and dispraise in turn.

Undoubtedly, courage pertaining the truth is the most meritorious type of jihād, as he said:

أَفْضَلُ الْجِهَادِ كَلِمَةُ حَقٍ عِنْدَ سُلْطَانٍ جَائِرٍ

"The most meritorious jihād is a statement of truth to an oppressive authority."

So when these two kinds of courage combine inside the heart of someone truly determined, who is free from whimsicalness and hypocrisy, then that will serve as the greatest aid for him in journeying to Allah (عَزَّوَجَلَّ) and gaining nearness to Him.

Also, it is not befitting for anyone who has attained such courage to search out peripheral people and riff-raff to contend with. Rather, he is to search out his match from his opponents, for indeed, dignity is found under the act of skirmishing with them. Furthermore, he is to listen to the advice of someone who is well-informed and experienced — meaning himself [i.e., Ibn al Qayyim (رَحِمَهُ ٱللَّهُ)]. He has knowledge about what all of humankind possessed of doctrines and opinions.

He swears by Allah that they do not possess anything more virtuous or beneficial than what they received from the Messenger (صَلَّىٰٱللَّهُعَلَيْهِوَسَلَّمَ) and that all that people profess beyond that is either: (1.) an innovated novelty that is baseless in Allah's religion, (2.) or it is a contrived fabrication invented by some liar, (3.) or it is a matter of research that aims to incite doubts and ambiguities about valid, readily-accepted beliefs, (4.) or it is an opinion transmitted from someone whose statement does not constitute a proof, being unsubstantiated by evidence.

52. The First Type of Courage

وَشَجَاعَةُ الفُرْسَانِ نَفْسُ الزُّهْدِ فِي ... نَفْسٍ، وَذَا مَحْذُورُ كُلِّ جَبَانِ

[52. /(239.)] The warrior's courage is precisely zuhd (abstemiousness) pertaining one's life, whereas that is something from which every coward is deprived.

'Abd al-Rahmān al-Sa'dī (رحمه الله) explains:

Meaning: that courage is *zuhd* [i.e., disinterestedness] regarding one's life. This requires further inspection. Instead, courage is strength of heart while zuhd regarding one's life is a necessitated requisite of that. So the author of the poem explained it as being its necessitated requisite.

Sālih al Fawzān (حفظه الله) explains:

He explained that the *zuhd* [i.e., disinterestedness] of the courageous person is having a disinterestedness pertaining life. This is extremely difficult for the coward. The coward fears death, but the courageous person goes forward without fearing death. If killed, then he is a martyr, and if he is victorious, then he is a *mujāhid* in Allah's path.

Muhammad bin Sālih al 'Uthaymīn (رحمه الله) explains:

You will hardly find this definition that he mentioned for courage mentioned in any book. The person's disinterest in his own self is courage. The fursān's (i.e., soldier; horseman) courage is precisely a disinterest pertaining life. When a person is disinterested in his own self, then death will not worry him because cowardice results from one stingily clinging to life, being afraid to advance forward lest that he be killed. So when he is disinterested in his own self, then losing his life will not worry him. This is courage. As such, you find the courageous person forgets himself when he advances. And he forgets everything else. The courage of the brave is disinterest in the self and the generosity of the generous is disinterest in wealth. Another type of disinterestedness then also comes into play, on account of which he said: "*The courage of the rulers and the scholars is disinterest in being praised by any person of falsehood.*"

53. The Second Type of Courage

وَشَجَاعَةُ الحُكَّامِ وَالْعُلَمَاءِ زُهْـ ... ـدٌ فِي الثَّنَا مِنْ كُلِّ ذِي بُطْلَانِ

[53. /(240.)] The courage of the rulers and the scholars is disinterest in being praised by any person of falsehood.

Sālih al Fawzān (حفظه الله) explains:

The *zuhd* of the scholars and rulers is their disinterestedness in praise and commendation. They do not want praise and commendation from people. Instead, they want to speak the truth, regardless of whether they are praised or dispraised. So they desire Allah's Face and do not intend to show-off to be seen or heard. When these qualities are combined: strong creed, strong weaponry, beneficial knowledge, courage without cowardice, disinterestedness in praise, and not looking at what people have to say — when these matters are combined, then a person can proceed upon *jihād* and battle.[21] Because, at that point, he is armed with faith, belief, knowledge, a disinterestedness about life or being praised. This is how the people of truth constantly and always procure victory — when these matters are combined.

Muhammad bin Sālih al-'Uthaymīn (رحمه الله) explains:

He said: "*the courage of the rulers...*" So likewise the courage of the rulers is that they not worry about the people's praise or criticism of them. They are to lead the people with Allah's book, even if the nations said that these people oppose human rights because they cut off the thief's hand and execute murderers. It is mandatory that the leaders — from the highest authority to everyone under him — do not worry about anyone and that they be disinterested in people's false praise of them.

The scholar's courage is having disinterestedness in being praised by people of falsehood, meaning that he does not flatter the people of falsehood. It does not matter to him whether they commend him or dispraise him. He says: I am knowledgeable and disseminate knowledge regardless of

[21] Spiritual preparedness is a required stipulation in legislated *jihād* and da'wah.

whether the people of falsehood praise or criticize me. So he is disinterested pertaining the people of falsehood praising him because when the people of falsehood see a scholar compromising with them, then they praise him, saying: "This scholar really understands matters. This is the scholar that is in agreement with every person." So they praise him in turn. So when he is disinterested in this praise, then he becomes a true scholar and is courageous. O Allah! Make us from them.

From that we say that scholars are of three categories: the community scholar, the scholar of the religion, and the scholar of the government.

The first is the scholar of the religion. He is the one who spreads the religion, the *sharī'ah* of Islām while being apathetic about those who oppose him and whether people commend or criticize him. This is the scholar of the religion who wishes to establish the *sharī'ah*. He is not worried by what people say about him such as: "This man is over-complicated," "This man is retrograde," "This person only knows a religion of the distant past." None of this bothers him.

The second is the community scholar, meaning that he looks at what the masses want. If he sees the masses interested in something — even though it may be *ḥarām* in the *sharī'ah* while people want it — then he goes into saying that this matter is *ḥalāl* and people cannot avoid it, we cannot refuse the people. So he gives *fatwā* to suit people's whims while trying to assign it some degree of permissiveness in the religion. So he distorts the texts for the sake of agreeing with people's whims.

If this person sees that praise will come by permitting usury-based banking, then he is the person who supposedly knows and understands the language and economics of today. So he tells the people to use *ribā* because the economy's survival is dependent on it. This person has noticed people's praise of him, thus he is apathetic about what opposes the religion.

When socialist propaganda appeared in Arab countries — which is really a predatory ideology of hunting down the wealthy — once it appeared, they started to produce evidence in its favor. They asserted that it is found in the *Qurān* and they validated it to such an extreme that they said about the Messenger (صَلَّى ٱللَّهُ عَلَيْهِ وَسَلَّمَ): "You are the Imām of the socialists!" From the most astonishing thing that I saw them use as a proof is what one of them said about Allah's statement (تَبَارَكَ وَتَعَالَىٰ) from the Qurān:

﴿ضَرَبَ لَكُم مَّثَلًا مِّنْ أَنفُسِكُمْ ۖ هَل لَّكُم مِّن مَّا مَلَكَتْ أَيْمَانُكُم مِّن شُرَكَاءَ فِي مَا رَزَقْنَاكُمْ فَأَنتُمْ فِيهِ سَوَاءٌ تَخَافُونَهُمْ كَخِيفَتِكُمْ أَنفُسَكُمْ ۚ﴾

"He presents to you an example from yourselves. Do you have among those whom your right hands possess any partners in what We have provided for you so that you are equal therein [and] would fear them as your fear of one another [within a partnership]?" [al-Rūm: 28].

He said that this is socialism between the slave and the master. That is (ostensibly) found in His saying: (تَبَارَكَ وَتَعَالَىٰ)

﴿هَل لَّكُم مِّن مَّا مَلَكَتْ أَيْمَانُكُم مِّن شُرَكَاءَ فِي مَا رَزَقْنَاكُمْ فَأَنتُمْ فِيهِ سَوَاءٌ﴾

"Do you have among those whom your right hands possess any partners in what We have provided for you so that you are equal therein?"

Allah's refuge is sought. Look at this distortion! What is the verse's meaning? It means: Are you partners with them such that you share in the partnership. The answer is in the negative as it is rhetorical and accompanied by implicit negation. Yet they made its response to be in the affirmative. They said that people are partners in three things [i.e., water, vegetation, and fire] and they designate the reason of their ruling to be that of shared need, thus [they claim that] people need socialism. People consist of different classes, some are who are exorbitantly wealthy, and some are who are destitute poor. So we need to assign this one's wealth to that one. However, in reality, they took the riches from the wealthy without helping the poor. The point is that the 'community scholar' is the one who looks at people's whims and wants, redirecting things to go in the manner that they wish.

The third is the scholar of the government who looks at what the government wants. If it wants something, he says: "This is permissible." "This has a considerable aspect weighing in its favor." Then he uses verses and aḥādīth, distorting them as evidence.

The scholars in reality — and we ask Allah (عَزَّوَجَلَّ) for protection — have a tremendous responsibility upon them. It is mandatory that they fear Allah (عَزَّوَجَلَّ) before fearing Allah's slaves.

So the courage of the fighter is disinterestedness in the self. The courage of the wealthy is disinterestedness in wealth. The courage of the scholar is disinterestedness in the commendation of the people of falsehood. The courage of the rulers is disinterestedness in people's praise or criticism. No one worries them.

In reality, these are guidelines. If when passing by them, you recorded them, taking note of them and then transferred them to a special notebook, that would prove to be of a great benefit and reference source for you. That is because they are guidelines that you won't find except in this book.

54. What Happens When These Two Combine?

فَإِذَا هُمَا اجْتَمَعَا لِقَلْبِ صَادِقٍ ... شَدَّتْ رَكَائِبُهُ إِلَى الرَّحْمَنِ

[54./(241.)] When these two combine within the heart of a person of genuineness, then his steeds will gallop quickly to al-Raḥmān.

'Abd al-Rahmān al-Sa'dī (رحمه الله) explains:

So their courage is *zuhd* regarding people's false praise. So he has explained combat courage and scholastic courage. Then he said: "*so when these combine in a genuine person's heart*" meaning when strength of heart and a disinterest in false praise are combined for a student of knowledge, then this person has been rightly guided, and in turn "*his steeds will gallop quickly to al-Raḥmān*" and how quickly will they arrive?!

Muhammad bin Sālih al 'Uthaymīn (رحمه الله) explains:

Meaning that when disinterestedness in living combines with disinterestedness in praise, then his mounts will gallop swiftly towards Allah and his intention will become Allah's face alone.

55. Selecting Well-Matched Opponents

وَاقْصِدْ إِلَى الأَقْرَانِ لاَ أَطْرَافِهَا ... فَالْعِزُّ تَحْتَ مَقَاتِلِ الأَقْرَانِ

[55. /(242.)] Search after well-matched opponents and not the outer flanks. Honor is found in fighting worthy opponents.

'Abd al-Rahmān al-Sa'dī (رحمه الله) explains:

Meaning that when you want to engage in a duel, whether it be physically or verbally, then search out your match and your own class and then duel against him. If you defeat such a person, you will achieve honor. As for peripheral people and the rabble who are not your match or in your class, then if you defeat them there is no honor or dignity in that because they are beneath you. And if they defeat you, then your goal would have been reversed.

Muhammad bin Sālih al 'Uthaymīn (رحمه الله) explains:

Meaning that when you contend, then do not go after random persons, but rather seek after well-matched opponents. Well-matched opponents are those comparable to you in courage. You are brave, so do not go towards the army's periphery — after persons lacking courage. That is because vanquishing them is easy. Instead, look for well-matched opponents that are like you and finish them off.

In similar fashion pertaining the scholars, then do not go after the commoners. Rather vanquish the scholar that is leading them to falsehood. Finish him off — of course meaning to do so with proof and evidence, not the sword. This is a behest from one well-acquainted with the affair, because if you want to do away with the falsehood of people then who do you search after? Do you go after a commoner, debating him about some doctrine? No, you go to the knowledgeable one. The common folk say, "*smash the snake's head and his tail will die.*" Yet if you hit his tail, it would not die.

Accordingly, he says, "*search after well-matched opponents, not the outer-ranks.*" Do not go at the periphery and side-ranks. You are unable to do anything with them. Instead, look at those well-matched who are knowledgeable like you and debate them until they are defeated in front of you, causing them to be defeated in front of their common-folk.

As for going after their common-folk, then never think of doing that. Twenty commoners could gather against you screaming at you or worse, one of them could be seized by jealousness and beat you. So do not speak to these ones. This is from the wisdoms that he has directed us toward.

56. - 58. Experienced Advice About People

وَاسْمَعْ نَصِيحَةَ مَنْ لَهُ خُبْرٌ بِمَا ... عِنْدَ الوَرَى مِنْ كَثْرَةِ الجَوَلَانِ

[56. /(243.)] Listen to the advice of one well-informed of what the people possess due to abundant encounters.

مَا عِنْدَهُمْ وَاللهِ خَيْرٌ غَيْرَ مَا ... أَخَذُوهُ عَمَّنْ جَاءَ بِالْقُرَآنِ

[57. /(244.)] By Allah! They have no good with them save that which they received from the one who came with the Qurān.

والكُلُّ بَعْدُ فَبِدْعَةٌ أَوْ فِرْيَةٌ ... أَوْ بَحْثُ تَشْكِيكٍ وَرَأْيُ فُلَانِ

[58. /(245.)] Everything else thereafter is innovation, fabrication or skeptical research and the opinion of fulān [i.e., so-and-so].

'Abd al-Rahmān al-Sa'dī (رَحِمَهُ ٱللَّهُ) explains:

"Listen to the advice of one well-informed of what the people have due to abundant encounters." He spoke the truth in this statement. There is none more knowledgeable after Shaykh al Islām (Ibn Taymiyyah) than him about their doctrines.

"Everything thereafter is innovation." Bid'ah is whatever is newly introduced into the religion in opposition to what the Prophet (صَلَّى ٱللَّهُ عَلَيْهِ وَسَلَّمَ) came with. A person could be an innovator without knowing that he has opposed the religion. *"Or fabrication,."* This is the innovation whose proponent knows that he has lyingly attributed something to the religion. *"Or skeptical research"* — this is by a person intentionally looking for a clear and unambiguous statement in an attempt to cause confusion about

it. What do you think about this or that? So he presents his research through doubts and ambiguities. This is forbidden, as there is a prohibition against asking unnecessarily-perplexing issues [*aghlūṭāt*]. This is similar to what Umar said to a man who had come from the people of Yemen asking: "What do you think about such-and-such, in the event that this or that happened?" So Umar responded: "Leave 'what do you think' in Yemen and ask about things that have happened."

As for beneficial research, then it is the type that explains and clarifies a given concept and is the type from which clear things of benefit branch off to further elucidate on what that thing necessitates and alludes to. Everything besides that is considered doubtful research.

Sālih al Fawzān (حفظه الله) explains:

He is saying to listen to the statement of someone who has experience about what people possess. The people do not possess anything of good except for what is from the Quran and the Sunnah. Everything else is misguidance and evanescence, amounting to nothing. This is what most people possess. It is either innovation, which is to seek nearness to Allah (عَزَّوَجَلَّ) with something He did not legislate. Or it is fabrication, which is lying on Allah and His Messenger (صَلَّى ٱللَّهُ عَلَيْهِ وَسَلَّمَ), as is found with the deviant sects. Or either it is speech without any benefit behind it. This is what most people have.

Muhammad bin Sālih al 'Uthaymīn (ﷺ) explains:

"Listen to the advice of one well-informed," meaning himself. Meaning that he has explored the doctrinal statements of the knowledgeable ones. It is not necessarily the case that he went to every scholar at his home, instead he ventured into the scholars' statements within their writings, carefully reflecting and acquainting himself with them.

"*By Allah! They have no good with them save that which they received from the one who came with the Qurān.*" This is said by the author out of fairness. He is saying that what good they do possess exists in the *Qurān*, yet most of what they possess is falsehood and evil. Since the good that they possess exists in the *Qurān*, then to where do I then refer? The answer is that I refer back to the *Qurān*. It does not bother me in the least if they agree with the *Qurān* in somethings and then I disprove other things that they possess which oppose the *Qurān*. That does not bother me.

"Everything else thereafter is innovation, fabrication or skeptical research and the opinion of fulān [i.e., so-and-so]."

He mentioned four categories:
The first is innovation that they introduced into Allah's religion of worship as pertains doctrine, statement, or practice.

The second is fabrication, meaning a lie that they tell about Allah.

The third is skeptical research in inquiries that they present for which they do not find answers. For this reason, some have said:

أَكْثَرُ النَّاسِ شَكًّا عِنْدَ الْمَوْتِ أَهْلُ الْكَلَام

"The people who have the most doubt at the time of death are the people of speculative theology."

O Allah! Protect us from that, O Rabb al 'Aalamīn [i.e. Nurturing Lord of the worlds]! Provide us with certainty during life and at the time of death.

The fourth is so-and-so's opinion. This is blind-following. So a person says that this one said and that one said.

So such people have nothing more than these four things: innovation, fabrication, skepticism, and blind-following.

X. Beautiful Patience, Clemency, and Ostracizing

Synopsis of Lines 59-63:

59. Reiteration of Boldness & Fearlessness

60. Sincere Boycotting

61. Beautiful Patience & Beautiful Clemency

62. Beautiful Ostracizing

63. The Preordainment of Guidance & Misguidance

X. Beautiful Patience, Clemency, and Ostracizing

فَاصْدَعْ بِأَمْرِ اللهِ لاَ تَخْشَ الوَرَى ... فِي اللهِ وَاخْشَاهُ تَفُزْ بِأَمَانِ

[59. /(246.)] Boldly proclaim your Lord's command and don't fear the people as pertains Allah. But rather fear Him so as to successfully attain safety.

وَاهْجُرْ وَلَوْ كُلَّ الوَرَى فِي ذَاتِهِ ... لاَ فِي هَوَاكَ وَنَخْوَةِ الشَّيْطَانِ

[60. /(247.)] Boycott, if you must, all of the people for His sake. However, do not do so for your own whims or out of the pride caused by Shayṭān.

وَاصْبِرْ بِغَيْرِ تَسَخُّطٍ وَشِكَايَةٍ ... وَاصْفَحْ بِغَيْرِ عِتَابِ مَنْ هُوَ جَانِ

[61. /(248.)] Be patient without being upset and complaining. Overlook without retribution against the offender.

وَاهْجُرْهُمُ الهَجْرَ الجَمِيلَ بِلَا أَذًى ... إِنْ لَمْ يَكُنْ بُدٌّ مِنَ الهِجْرَانَ

[62. /(249.)] Boycott them with beautiful ostracizing, without any abusiveness — in the instance where boycotting is unavoidable.

وَانْظُرْ إِلَى الأَقْدَارِ جَارِيَةً بِمَا ... قَدْ شَاءَ مِنْ غَيٍّ وِمِنْ إِيْمَانِ

[63. /(250.)] Look at the preordainments occurring just as He willed pertaining misguidance and faith.

Synopsis of Lines 59-63

Muhammad Khalīl Harrās(رَحِمَهُ ٱللَّهُ) summarizes:

Boldly proclaiming a matter *(al-ṣada')* means publicizing and announcing it, as Allah said to His Prophet (صَلَّىٰ ٱللَّهُ عَلَيْهِ وَسَلَّمَ):

﴿ فَٱصْدَعْ بِمَا تُؤْمَرُ ﴾

"Therefore proclaim openly (Allah's Message Islamic Monotheism) that which you are commanded." [al Ḥijr: 94]

The meaning is publicly declare the statement of truth and do not hide it out of fearing people, for indeed, Allah (عَزَّوَجَلَّ) is more deserving that you fear Him. By fearing Him, success is achieved in full tranquility and safety.

If proclaiming the word of truth requires, then oppose all of the people and boycott them for Allah's sake, not for the sake of your personal desires and the pridefulness from *Shayṭān*. Do not allow that to weigh heavily upon you. You are to react with beautiful patience without being weary or complaining, and you are to pardon in a beautiful fashion without pursuing recourse against those who abused or committed offense against you.

When you are forced to boycott and avoid people then make your boycotting beautiful, not accompanied by abusiveness. You are to look at what Allah (عَزَّوَجَلَّ) has predestined and how His Will relates to how people differ in deviance and faith.

59. Reiteration of Boldness & Fearlessness

فَاصْدَعْ بِأَمْرِ اللهِ لاَ تَخْشَ الوَرَى ... فِي اللهِ وَاخْشَاهُ تَفُزْ بِأَمَانِ

[59. /(246.)] Boldly proclaim Allah's commandment and don't fear the people as pertains Allah. But rather fear Him so as to successfully achieve safety.

Muhammad bin Sālih al 'Uthaymīn (رحمه الله) explains:

His statement, "*boldly proclaim Allah's commandment*" is based on His saying (تَبَارَكَ وَتَعَالَى):

﴿فَاصْدَعْ بِمَا تُؤْمَرُ﴾

"Therefore proclaim openly (Allah's Message Islamic Monotheism) that which you are commanded." [al Ḥijr: 94]

"*Boldly proclaim*" means clarify it with a singular explanation whose strength of explanation and proclaiming could split stone. His statement, "*do not fear the people*" is taken from His saying (تَبَارَكَ وَتَعَالَى):

﴿فَلَا تَخْشَوُا النَّاسَ وَاخْشَوْنِ﴾

"So do not fear the people but fear Me" [al Mā'idah: 44]

His statement, "*but rather fear Him so as to successfully achieve safety*" means that once you have done that, namely, once you have boldly proclaimed the truth and have feared Allah (عَزَّوَجَلَّ) to the exclusion of all else, you will successfully achieve safety.

So the author is saying: It is mandatory that a person boldly proclaims the truth, fearing nothing but Allah (عَزَّوَجَلَّ). For indeed safety rests within fearing Allah (عَزَّوَجَلَّ). The real height of fearfulness is found within fearing people. Whoever fears Allah (عَزَّوَجَلَّ) will be feared by the people and whoever fears the people will be stepped on by the people.

60. Sincere Boycotting

وَاهْجُرْ وَلَوْ كُلَّ الوَرَى فِي ذَاتِهِ ... لاَ فِي هَوَاكَ وَنَخْوَةِ الشَّيْطَانِ

[60./(247.)] Boycott, if you must, all of the people for His sake. However, do not do so for your own whims or out of the pride caused by Shayṭān.

Aḥmad bin ʿIsā al-Najdī (رَحِمَهُ ٱللَّهُ) explains:

"*The nakhwa of Shayṭah*" *Nakhwa* is arrogance and self-exultation. It is said that a person has done this who has boasted and behaved haughtily as was stated by the author of *Mukhtār al-Ṣiḥāḥ*.

Muḥammad bin Sāliḥ al ʿUthaymīn (رَحِمَهُ ٱللَّهُ) explains:

Meaning boycott whoever opposes the truth — even if that be all people — for Allah's sake. His saying, "*do not do so for your own whims*" means do not boycott them in defense of your personal feelings. As for his saying, "*or out of (nakhwah) pridefulness caused by Shayṭān,*" then *nakhwah* is being indignant for Allah (عَزَّوَجَلَّ), for Allah's sake, even if that included your father and mother, boycott them for Allah's sake. However, be as Allah (تَبَارَكَوَتَعَالَىٰ) said:

﴿ وَصَاحِبْهُمَا فِي الدُّنْيَا مَعْرُوفًا ﴾

"But accompany them in [this] world with appropriate kindness." [Luqmān: 15]

61. Beautiful Patience & Beautiful Clemency

وَاصْبِرْ بِغَيْرِ تَسَخُّطٍ وَشِكَايَةٍ ... وَاصْفَحْ بِغَيْرِ عِتَابِ مَنْ هُوَ جَانِ

[61./(248.)] Be patient without being upset and complaining. Overlook without retribution against the offender.

'Abd al-Rahmān al-Sa'dī (رَحِمَهُ ٱللَّهُ) explains:

This is a precious benefit that clarifies what is found in the *Quran* as pertains beautiful patience (*al-ṣabr al jamīl*) and beautiful pardoning (*al-ṣafḥ al jamīl*). The author explained it in an extensive manner.

He said: "*Boycott them with beautiful ostracizing,*" which is that which does not entail being upset with the ostracized party or complaining to people about them. As for complaining to the Creator, then this does not contradict beautiful patience, rather it is commendable, as Allah (تَبَارَكَوَتَعَالَىٰ) said about Ya'qūb:

﴿ قَالَ إِنَّمَا أَشْكُو بَثِّي وَحُزْنِي إِلَى اللَّهِ ﴾

"He said, 'I only complain of my suffering and my grief to Allah.'" [Yusuf: 86].

Likewise, it is just as the best of the creation said:

اللَّهُمَّ لَكَ الْحَمْدُ وَإِلَيْكَ الْمُشْتَكَى

"Oh Allah! All praise is due to You and all complaining is to You alone."

Muhammad bin Sālih al 'Uthaymīn (رَحِمَهُ ٱللَّهُ) explains:

"*Be patient*" for Allah to judge what befalls you of abuse and harm. As for his statement, "*without being upset and complaining,*" then do not be upset with your heart and do not complain with your tongue. As for his statement, "*overlook without retribution against the offender,*" then the meaning of *al-ṣafḥ* (overlooking) is to turn away from that thing. It is linguistically derived from *ṣafḥa al 'unuq* [i.e., the side of the neck], because when a person turns away, then the side of his neck is exposed. The meaning is that you are to look away from these people "*without retribution against the offender.*" However, you must speak the truth.

This entails an indication to what repudiates the method employed by some people, even by some scholars. Whenever someone opposes their opinion, even if that happens out of *ijtihād* (a diligent effort to conclude what is correct), then he initiates a terrible revilement against them. From those who employed this way was Ibn Ḥazm (رَحِمَهُ ٱللَّهُ). Woe be to anyone who opposed him. He would revile them in a terrible manner, and this is a great error.[22] So it is upon you to be patient and to invite to Allah (عَزَّوَجَلَّ) in truth without being upset and without retribution.

62. Beautiful Ostracizing

وَاهْجُرْهُمُ الهَجْرَ الجَمِيلَ بِلَا أَذىً ... إِنْ لَمْ يَكُنْ بُدٌّ مِنَ الهِجْرَانِ

[62. /(249.)] Boycott them with beautiful ostracizing, without abusiveness — in the instance where boycotting is unavoidable.

Ahmad bin 'Isā al-Najdī (رَحِمَهُ ٱللَّهُ) explains:

The author of the poem stated in Badā'i al Fawā'id:

> I heard Shaykh al Islām saying that Allah (عَزَّوَجَلَّ) mentioned beautiful patience, beautiful clemency, and beautiful ostracizing. Beautiful patience is that which in unaccompanied by complaining. Beautiful ostracizing is that which is not accompanied by abuse. Beautiful clemency is that which is not accompanied by rebuke.

[22] T.N.: Shaykh 'Uthaymīn is mentioning something well-known as a cautionary point. He is not reviling Ibn Ḥazm. May Allah (عَزَّوَجَلَّ) have mercy on Ibn Ḥazm (d. 456 h.), he admitted this about himself, recognized it as a personal flaw, and openly discussed how he actively struggled to remove this trait, seeking Allah's assistance in doing so. See: *al akhlāq wal-sayr fī mudāwāh al-nufūs*, pp. 33-36. Dār al Afāq al Jadīda, Beirut; 2nd edition (1399 h./1979)

'Abd al-Rahmān al-Sa'dī (رَحِمَهُ ٱللَّهُ) explains:

As pertains beautiful pardoning, then it is that which contains no retribution against the person who mistreated you. As for beautiful boycotting, then it contains no abuse of the ostracized party.

Since the first two are unrestrictedly commendable, he did not qualify them with any modifier, contrary to the matter of boycotting, which he qualifies with the modifier "*so long as ostracizing is unavoidable.*" Meaning: do not boycott anyone unless there is a resulting preponderant benefit that outweighs the harm of boycotting. So it is better to refrain from it. The Prophet (صَلَّىٰٱللَّهُعَلَيْهِوَسَلَّمَ) was careful about ensuring the benefit in doing so. He boycotted the three men, and in other instances, despite the fact that the hypocrites were worse than them, but since there was a harm in boycotting the hypocrites, he refrained from it.

Muhammad bin Sālih al 'Uthaymīn (رَحِمَهُ ٱللَّهُ) explains:

As for his statement, "***boycott them in a beautiful manner,***" then beautiful boycotting is boycotting without abusiveness just as beautiful patience is patience without complaining.

His statement, "*so long as boycotting is unavoidable*" means do not boycott them unless boycotting must be done. In that case, then boycott them without abusiveness.

This shows the tolerance of Ibn al Qayyim (رَحِمَهُ ٱللَّهُ) in these sorts of matters, contrary to what some people do today out of protective jealousy and emotionalism. You find him being extreme in arguing with, boycotting, and isolating others. And this is not from the way of the *Salaf*.

Sālih al Fawzān (حفظه الله) explains:

We have three things here that Allah (عَزَّوَجَلَّ) mentioned in His Book: beautiful patience, beautiful clemency, and beautiful ostracizing. It is binding for the student of knowledge and the caller to Allah to adorn himself with these things.

Beautiful patience is that which does not entail complaining to people. Instead, he complains to Allah (عَزَّوَجَلَّ). Accordingly, Ya'qūb said:

﴿قَالَ إِنَّمَا أَشْكُو بَثِّي وَحُزْنِي إِلَى اللَّهِ﴾

"He said, 'I only complain of my suffering and my grief to Allah.'" [Yusuf: 86]. This is despite him having said:

﴿فَصَبْرٌ جَمِيلٌ﴾

"So patience is most fitting" [Yusuf: 83].

Complaining to Allah (عَزَّوَجَلَّ) does not contradict patience. The only such thing that contradicts patience is complaining to people.

Beautiful clemency is that which does not entail rebuke. If it is accompanied by rebuke then it is not the beautiful sort of clemency.

Beautiful ostracizing is that which does not entail abuse or selfish revenge.

These three matters are mentioned in the Qurān. Shaykh al Islām Ibn Taymiyyah has a standalone treatise on these three things *Pertaining Beautiful Patience, Clemency, and Ostracizing.*

63. The Preordainment of Guidance & Misguidance

وَانْظُرْ إِلَى الأَقْدَارِ جَارِيَةً بِمَا ... قَدْ شَاءَ مِنْ غَيٍّ وِمِنْ إِيْمَانِ

[63./(250.)] Look at the preordainments occurring just as He willed pertaining misguidance and faith.

'Abd al-Rahmān al-Sa'dī (رحمه الله) explains:

This entails an explanation that distinguishes the universal law of predestination from religious, legislative law. This is because concepts such as *al ḥukm* (judgment), *al qaḍā'* (ordainment), *al irādah* (intent), *al idhn* (permission), *al kitāb* (writing or prescribing), *al-taḥrīm* (forbidding, depriving) and *kalimāt* (divine words), each have types that are indicative of what is universal and predestined as well as that which is legislative and religious in nature.

Meaning: so look at how the creation is categorized into the obedient and the disobedient, the successful and the wretched, and the righteous and the wicked.

Muhammad bin Sālih al 'Uthaymīn (رَحِمَهُ ٱللَّهُ) explains:

Meaning that Allah (عَزَّوَجَلَّ) willed that. So look at how Allah's preordainments occur pertaining misguidance and faith, just as He wills.

This man is righteous and pious while another is sinful and miserable. Who preordained that? Certainly it was Allah (عَزَّوَجَلَّ), but it did not happen by force, rather the human has volition. However, when al-Rabb (عَزَّوَجَلَّ) sees deviance from the slave, then He causes their hearts to deviate, just as He (تَبَارَكَ وَتَعَالَىٰ) said:

﴿ فَلَمَّا زَاغُوا أَزَاغَ اللَّهُ قُلُوبَهُمْ ﴾

"And when they deviated, Allah caused their hearts to deviate." [al-Ṣaff: 5]

So look at Allah's predestinations and you will find one man who is intelligent with ample money, who charitably spends much, with good opinion formation, yet you find that he is a disbeliever. You find another man much less than him in those things, yet he is a believer. So look at Allah's preordainments, how they happen as He wills. But is this purely Divine Will, or is it Divine Will due to a Divine Wisdom? The answer is in the affirmative, that this is Divine Will due to a Divine Wisdom.

XI. Looking at People from Two Perspectives

Synopsis of Lines 64-68:

64. & 65. Having a Balance Outlook at People

66. The Second Perspective

67. & 68. Weeping out of Fearfulness of Allah

XI. Looking at People from Two Perspectives

وَاجْعَل لِقَلْبِكَ مُقْلَتَيْنِ كِلَاهُمَا ... بِالحَقِّ فِي ذَا الخَلْقِ نَاظِرَتَانِ

[64. /(251.)] Assign two eyes to your heart, both of which view the creation by means of the truth.

فَانْظُرْ بِعَيْنِ الحُكْمِ وَارْحَمْهُمْ بِهَا ... إِذْ لَا تُرَدُّ مَشِيئَةُ الدَّيَّانِ

[65. /(252.)] Look through the eye of what he preordained and feel mercy towards them thereby, because nothing can refuse the will of al-Dayyān.

وَانْظُر بِعَيْنِ الأَمْرِ وَاحْمِلْهُمْ عَلَى ... أَحْكَامِهِ فَهُمَا إِذَنْ نَظَرَانِ

[66. /(253.)] Also, look with the eye of Divine commandment and treat bind them to His laws. For these are two different viewpoints.

وَاجْعَلْ لِوَجْهِكَ مُقْلَتَيْنِ كِلَاهُمَا ... مِنَ خَشْيَةِ الرَّحْمَنِ بَاكِيَتَانِ

[67. /(254.)] Make sure that in your face you have two eyes, both of which weep out of fearing al-Raḥmān.

لَوْ شَاءَ رَبُّكَ كُنْتَ أَيْضًا مِثْلَهُمْ ... فَالْقَلْبُ بَيْنَ أَصَابِعِ الرَّحْمَنِ

[68. /(255.)]Had your Lord willed, you would have also been like them, for the heart is between al-Raḥmān's Fingers.

Synopsis of Lines 64-68

Muhammad Khalīl Harrās(رَحِمَهُ ٱللَّهُ) summarizes:

Since Allah (عَزَّوَجَلَّ) has (1.) set predestination in motion upon the servants and has judged what He willed of disbelief and faith to transpire pertaining them, and (2.) since He has commanded them all with faith and obedience, then it is mandatory for a person to look at the creation in accordance to these two different outlooks.

He looks with one eye at the execution of divine judgment and predestination, thus having pity and empathy for them due to his knowledge that Allah's judgment and preordainment cannot be rejected or deflected. He also looks with the eye of divine commandment that is applicable to all who are responsible for their actions. So he struggles against them in that regard, being stern against them so as to bind them to Allah's commandment and religious law. These are two different outlooks. It does not necessitate the type of difference that constitutes a contradiction. The perspective of each differs from that of the other and it would only be a contradiction if the two were viewed to be one and the same.

As such, it is necessary for the worshipper that when looking at people's differing pertaining guidance and misguidance to shed tears from his eyes weeping out of fearing Allah (عَزَّوَجَلَّ) and being grateful for the blessing of guidance and tawfīq. Had Allah (عَزَّوَجَلَّ) so willed, then he would have also been like them, for indeed, the hearts are between two of Allah's fingers, who turns them as He wills. Accordingly, the Prophet (ﷺ) frequently supplicated in his invocation, saying:

اللّٰهُمَّ يا مقلِّبَ القُلُوبِ ثبِّت قَلْبي على دينك

"O Allah! Changer of the hearts! Make my heart firm upon your religion."

64. & 65. Having a Balance Outlook at People

وَاجْعَل لِقَلْبِكَ مُقْلَتَيْنِ كِلَاهُمَا ... بِالحَقِّ فِي ذَا الخَلْقِ نَاظِرَتَانِ

[64. /(251.)] Assign two eyes to your heart, both of which view the creation by means of the truth.

فَانْظُرْ بِعَيْنِ الحُكْمِ وَارْحَمْهُمْ بِهَا ... إِذْ لَا تُرَدُّ مَشِيئَةُ الدَّيَّانِ

[65. /(252.)] Look through an eye at divine rule [i.e., predestiny] and feel mercy towards them thereby, because nothing can refuse the will of al-Dayyān.

'Abd al-Rahmān al-Sa'dī (رحمه الله) explains:

Once you have looked at this angle, then "*assign two eyes to your heart,*" which are conceptual, "*both of which look at the creation by means of the truth.*"

He said: "*Look through the eye of what He preordained and feel mercy towards them thereby,*" — as pertains the universal predestined type. "*Because nothing can refuse the will of al-Dayyān.*" This is because the universe, all that it contains, and all actions of the slaves, whether they be obedience or disobedience, are created, predestined, willed, and written by Allah (عَزَّوَجَلَّ).

Muhammad bin Sālih al 'Uthaymīn (رَحِمَهُ ٱللَّهُ) explains:

Make your heart have two eyes that look at the creation from two perspectives. "*Look through the eye at divine rule [i.e., predestiny] and feel mercy towards them thereby, because nothing can refuse the will of al-Dayyān.*" His saying, "*so look with an eye at divine rule*" meaning the universal law pertaining divine predestiny, namely, how Allah (عَزَّوَجَلَّ) judged that misguidance would be the lot of such people.

His saying, "*and feel mercy towards them thereby*" with this eye. {Look at} how Allah (عَزَّوَجَلَّ) set these unfortunate people astray so that they remain bewildered, not building their situation upon any principle and not having a creed. So you pity them and say: All praise is for Allah (عَزَّوَجَلَّ) who gave me a degree of virtue above them. This is the first perspective.

66. The Second Perspective

وَانْظُرْ بِعَيْنِ الأَمْرِ وَاحْمِلْهُمْ عَلَى ... أَحْكَامِهِ فَهُمَا إِذَنْ نَظَرَانِ

[66. /(253.)] Also, look with an eye at divine commandment and bind them to His laws.
For these are two different viewpoints.

'Abd al-Raḥmān al-Sa'dī (رَحِمَهُ ٱللَّهُ) explains:

Along with that "*Also, look with an eye at divine commandment,*" — as pertains the religious legislative type, "*and bind them to His laws.*" So you[23] execute the murderer and exact the legislative punishments upon the adulterer, thief, the one who drinks intoxicants, etc. Also, you are to bind them to enacting the commandments and abstaining from the prohibitions. "*For these are two different viewpoints,*" both of which are correct. By doing so, you will be spared from the narrow perspective of the *Qadariyyah* who assert that the servant is the one who brings his actions into existence, creating and willing them to happen, while saying that Allah (عَزَّوَجَلَّ) did not create these things or will for them to occur. Likewise, there is the narrow perspective of the *Jabriyyah* sect who say that Allah (عَزَّوَجَلَّ) is the doer of the servants actions Who created him with them, asserting thereby that they are not the actions of the slave except in a figurative sense. These are two contradictory extremes, whereas Ahl al-Sunnah constitute a centrist moderation between the two.

Muḥammad bin Ṣāliḥ al 'Uthaymīn (رَحِمَهُ ٱللَّهُ) explains:

As for the second perspective, then he says: "*Also, look with the eye of commandment and treat them according to His laws. For these are two different viewpoints.*" His statement, "*treat them according to its laws,*" means bind them to them as being responsible parties and do not be taken aback by the blame of the blamers

[23] T.N.: Meaning the legal Muslim authorities in a Muslim nation.

as pertains Allah's religion. So, henceforth, we have two perspectives:

The first perspective is that you look at them with one eye on predestination, which necessitates mercy and pity for them, as well as having a heavy-heartedness for them while we praise Allah that he spared us from that with which he tested them. That is because these are Allah's preordainments. So when you look at a person who is forsaken — and Allah's refuge is sought. Then you are to look at him and say that he is unfortunate, look at how he is obstructed from guidance and instead has followed whimsicalness and ruin!

The second perspective is the eye of the religion. Based on this perspective you are to treat people according to the law, even if that requires corporal punishment or detention. Allah (تَبَارَكَ وَتَعَالَىٰ) said:

﴿وَلَا تَأْخُذْكُم بِهِمَا رَأْفَةٌ فِي دِينِ اللَّهِ﴾

"Let not pity withhold you in their case, in a punishment prescribed by Allah." [al-Nūr: 2]

So He said, "*Also, look with an eye at divine commandment and treat them according to His law.*" However, when having an eye on predestiny, then have pity on them and empathize with their pain.

Al-Shāfi'ī (رَحِمَهُ ٱللَّهُ) said:

حُكْمِي فِي أَهْلِ الكلام: أَنْ يَضْرَبُوا بَالْجَرِيدِ وَالنِّعَال وَيُطَاف بِهِمْ فِي الْقَبَائِلِ وَالْعَشَائِرِ، وَيُقَالَ: هَذَا جَزَاءُ مَنْ تَرَكَ الْكِتَابَ وَالسُّنَّةَ وَأَقْبَلَ عَلَى الْكَلَامِ

"My judgement upon the people of speculative theology is that they be beaten with twisted date palm leaves and sandals, and that they be paraded around to the tribes and families while it is declared that this is the recompense of whoever abandons the Book and the Sunnah while focusing on speculative theology."

Which of the outlooks is this? The answer is the second.

Shaykh al Islām (رَحِمَهُ ٱللَّهُ) said in *al Fatwā al Ḥamawiyyah*:

Al 'Alīm (i.e., Allah the All-Knowing) knows that they come with that which makes them deserving of that which al-Shāfi'ī said.

This is when we look at them with an eye at divine commandment. However, were you to look at them with an eye at predestiny, then you would pity them. You would say: Allah (عَزَّوَجَلَّ) is free from imperfection! Look at how He decreed the straying of these people! Although they may be intelligent people having virtuous character traits, and although they might be people practicing many acts of worship and having reverential humility they strayed in creed. There is no doubt that this is from Divine Justice. When you look at them from this angle, then you will be at the height of diligence in working to bind them to the religion. That is because whoever pities someone for not having something must strive to procure that for them.

Sālih al Fawzān (حفظه الله) explains:

He is saying that you are to look at what takes place with people with two perspectives:

A perspective from the angle of predestination and preordainment. Through that you will know that whatever Allah (عَزَّوَجَلَّ) predestined of their actions must happen, so do not blame them over predestination and preordainment. Another perspective is that of the religion, namely, that He commanded them with good and forbade them from evil. Based on that you blame them for acts of disobedience and opposition, while ordering them with acts of obedience. The person looking from the first perspective alone, then this is the perspective of the *Jabriyyah*. Whoever looks exclusively at the servants' actions — the second perspective — without looking and predestination and preordainment, then this is the perspective of the *Qadariyyah*. As for Ahl al-Sunnah, then they look at both perspectives, a perspective pertaining predestination and preordainment and another perspective pertaining what Allah (عَزَّوَجَلَّ) ordered and forbade. He gave people the ability and the wherewithal to choose either of their own volition — they could either do good or evil predicated on their choosing and wanting. So do not look from a single perspective at preordainment alone, nor at divine commandment alone, rather look at the two matters combined.

Ahmad bin 'Isā al-Najdī (رَحِمَهُ ٱللَّهُ) explains:

The author's intent by these verses of poetry is to explain Allah's universal law of predestiny as well as that law pertaining to religious commandment. For indeed, all actions of creatures — all acts of obedience and disobedience, belief and unbelief — are not outside of the universal law of the Rabb pertaining preordainment. For certainly Allah (عَزَّوَجَلَّ) created all things through His Power and His Will. However, alongside that, the law pertaining religious commandment must be looked at. So the meaning of his speech is that when you have looked at the creation with the eye at the divine rule (of universal preordainment), then you will feel merciful towards them, because Allah's Will cannot be stopped. Whatever He wills transpires and what He does not will does not happen. However, alongside that, look with an eye at divine commandment and bind them to that. Meaning enact the punishment for the fornicator, the thief, and the slanderer and execute the murderer and what is similar to that as Allah (عَزَّوَجَلَّ) and the Messenger (صَلَّىٱللَّهُعَلَيْهِوَسَلَّمَ) commanded.

The author [i.e., Ibn al Qayyim (رَحِمَهُٱللَّهُ)] said in *Madārij al-Sālikīn* about what the mystics call *al fanā'* (obliteration of distinctions):

> The basis of this *fanā'* [i.e., self-obliteration] is becoming fully engrossed in *Tawḥīd al-Rububiyyah* which is: looking at Allah's exclusivity in originating, owning, and creating all things; and that there is nothing in existence except for what He has willed and made to exist. So such a person witnesses the commonality shared by all of creation pertaining: Allah's creation of them all, His willing that they exist, His Power over them, His all-encompassing Providence, and His nurturing Lordship over all. However, they do so without witnessing the distinction within it all as pertains Allah (عَزَّوَجَلَّ) loving some things while hating others, His commanding some things while forbidding others, and His endowing some people with supportive guardianship while having enmity for others.
>
> Such a person does not see any distinction within the whole, which is: the distinction between Creation [i.e., *al qadar*] and Commandment within all that is part of the concept of

Rububiyah [i.e., Lordship]; the distinction of what being the sole Deity necessitates [i.e., that He be worshipped alone] within all that is part of the concept of *Rububiyyah*; (3.) the distinction of *al irādah al-dīniyyah* (religious requirement) within all that is part of the concept of *al irādah al kawniyyah* (universal will); the distinction of what He loves and is pleased with amidst the fuller concept of what He has predestined and preordained.

Such a person does not see any abundance in existence, which includes: the abundance of the meanings of (Allah's) Beautiful Names and Lofty Attributes and what they necessitate of effects as relates the essence of the Single Being to whom they are attributed. So they do not observe the significance of the Lord's Names and Attributes as pertains the uniqueness of His Being. He is Allah (عَزَّوَجَلَّ), whom none deserve worship as a deity besides. He is al-Raḥmān, al-Raḥīm, al Malik, al Quddūs, al-Salām, al Mu'min, al Muhaymin, al 'Azīz, al Jabbār, al Mutakabbir. Every name entails an attribute and every attribute has a distinct ruling. So He is One in essence while having many Names and Attributes. So this constitutes abundance of meaning within singularity of essence (*kathra fī waḥda*).

The distinction between what He ordered and forbade, between what He loves and hates, and between His allies and enemies all constitute a distinction within a collective whole (*tafriqa fī jam'*). Whoever cannot accommodate the capacity to observe these aforementioned four matters,[24] then He is not from the Allah's choice allies who know Him. Even if his observance of this was constricted while still ceding its veracity, then he would be a deficient believer. However, if he denies it, in whole or in part, then that is either out of explicit disbelief or due to misinterpretation, such as denying: the distinction between command and prohibition; their connection to preordainment and predestiny; or harmonizing the abundant meanings of the Names and Attributes with the singularity of Divine Essence.

Let the intelligent sojourner afford this topic due contemplation, and let him know its status. *For indeed it is the crossroads of the creations' diverging paths and the source of their disunity.* **Its intricacies and principles have now been exacted and standardized for your benefit.** And Providential Guidance is only through Allah (عَزَّوَجَلَّ).

---

[24] These first of these four matters is related to recognizing abundance in singularity, which is contrary to the creed of the mystics who cannot harmonize:

(1.) Between an abundance of meanings pertaining Divine Names and Attributes within the singularity of Divine Essence.

Likewise, they cannot harmonize or reconcile between three other matters that are related to recognizing distinction amongst a collective whole, which includes:

(2.) The distinction between what He ordered and forbade.

(3.) The distinction between what He loves and hates.

(4.) The distinction between His enemies and allies.

67. & 68. Weeping out of Fearfulness of Allah

وَاجْعَلْ لِوَجْهِكَ مُقْلَتَيْنِ كِلَاهُمَا ... مِنْ خَشْيَةِ الرَّحْمَنِ بَاكِيَتَانِ

[67. /(254.)] Make sure that in your face you have two eyes, both of which weep out of fearing al-Raḥmān.

لَوْ شَاءَ رَبُّكَ كُنْتَ أَيْضًا مِثْلَهُمْ ... فَالْقَلْبُ بَيْنَ أَصَابِعِ الرَّحْمَنِ

[68. /(255.)]Had your Lord willed, you would have also been like them, for the hearts are between al-Raḥmān's Fingers.

'Abd al-Rahmān al-Sa'dī (رَحِمَهُ ٱللَّهُ) explains:

He said, "*make sure that your face has two eyes,*" meaning two physical eyes, "*both of which weep out of fearing Allah.*" So the author has directed to have fear and take lesson about how Allah (عَزَّوَجَلَّ) changes the hearts. As such, he then said, *"had your Lord willed, you would have also been like them, for the hearts are between al-Raḥmān's Fingers."*

"Had Allah willed, you would also have been like them." He means (like) the Jahmiyyah. *"For certainly the hearts are between al-Raḥmān"* as is mentioned in the ḥadīth. The Prophet (صَلَّى ٱللَّهُ عَلَيْهِ وَسَلَّمَ) frequently supplicated with the following invocation:

يَا مُقَلِّبَ الْقُلُوبِ ! ثَبِّتْ قَلْبِي عَلَى دِينِكَ

"Oh changer of hearts! May my heart firm on your religion."

Sālih al Fawzān (حفظه الله) *explains:*

He is saying that if your Lord had so willed, then you would have also been like that, meaning that you would have been like these unbelievers and like the sinful people. So do not praise yourself, but instead praise Allah (عَزَّوَجَلَّ) who spared you from that with which He tested them. Fear that you will deviate like they did because the hearts are between the fingers of al-Raḥmān. So one does not feel safe from misguidance pertaining oneself no matter what he has reached of knowledge and piety. So he does not feel safe for himself from deviance because once he feels safe for himself, then it is most likely that he will be afflicted. So he looks at those who are trialled and praises Allah (عَزَّوَجَلَّ) for well-being while fearing that what struck them might strike him, because what struck them was only by the preordainment and predestining of Allah (عَزَّوَجَلَّ). Had Allah (عَزَّوَجَلَّ) so willed, He could have made him like them.

Muhammad bin Sālih al 'Uthaymīn (رحمه الله) *explains:*

It has preceded that one is to assign two eyes to the heart by which to view the creation: an eye on predestiny and an eye on the religion. As for (the eyes in one's) face, then he says, "*make sure that in your face you have two eyes, both of which weep out of fearing al-Raḥmān.*"

"*Muqlatayn*" means two eyeballs: make your two eyes weep out of fearing Allah (عَزَّوَجَلَّ). There is something fitting to say at every instance. In the instance of worship and pleadingly supplicating Allah (عَزَّوَجَلَّ), then compel the eye to weep, because the situation requires it. In the situation of debating and defending the truth, then do not do so, because your opponent may view this as an instance of weakness. So there is something appropriate to be said of every situation. The knight upon his horse does not cry like someone does while prostrating in a state of reverential humility for Allah (عَزَّوَجَلَّ). What al Qaḥṭānī (رَحِمَهُ ٱللَّهُ) says in his Nuniyah has the same meaning as this:

يا حبّذا عينان في غسق الدجى   من خشية الرحمن باكيتان

"How commendably loved would it be to have two eyes in the pitch darkness (i.e., of the night) that weep out of fearing al-Raḥmān."

Where is the person from us who practices that? Rather, most people today sleep until the morning and if they get up in the darkness of the night, then they weep very little. However, it is rare in our time that one has two eyes that weep in the pitch darkness out of fear of al-Raḥmān. We ask Allah (عَزَّوَجَلَّ) to make ourselves and yourselves from that few.

So a person should have a connection with Allah (عَزَّوَجَلَّ), crying during prostration and while standing in prayer out of fearing Allah (عَزَّوَجَلَّ). Whenever he reflects on Allah's verses, that should cause fear of Him so that his heart softens. If you do not soften your heart, it will remain hard. That can be caused by the lusciousness and ornamentation of temporal life and one's associates, as well as similar things. All or some of this can cause the heart's hardness. So you must afford care to your heart so as to soften it. The best thing by which to soften it is reciting Allah's Book with concentration and contemplation.

For indeed, that softens the heart, as Ibn 'Abd al Qawī (رَحِمَهُ ٱللَّهُ) said:

وَحَافِظِ عَلَى دَرْسِ الْقُرآنِ فَإِنَّهُ يُلَيِّنُ قَلْبًا قَاسِيًا مِثْلَ جَلْمَدِ

Diligently attend to studying the Qurān, for indeed it softens the heart that is as hard as a rock.

This is proven by His saying (تَبَارَكَ وَتَعَالَى):

﴿لَوْ أَنزَلْنَا هَٰذَا الْقُرْآنَ عَلَىٰ جَبَلٍ لَّرَأَيْتَهُ خَاشِعًا مُّتَصَدِّعًا مِّنْ خَشْيَةِ اللَّهِ﴾

"If We had sent down this Qur'an upon a mountain, you would have seen it humbled and coming apart from fear of Allah." [al Ḥashr: 21]

Had your Lord willed, you would have also been like them, for the hearts are between al-Raḥmān's Fingers.

He said the truth. Had Allah (عَزَّوَجَلَّ) so willed, then you would be like them. Meaning that you would be like these deviant ones who strayed from the truth — because you are human and just another person who reads as they read and reflects and they reflect. Had Allah (عَزَّوَجَلَّ) so willed he could have ordained misguidance for you.

So praise Allah (عَزَّوَجَلَّ) for the blessing of guidance and know the degree of Allah's favor upon you. Know that He has conferred the greatest, weightiest blessing upon you, because had He so willed, then He could have made your heart deviate — and Allah's refuge is sought. So do not be amazed with yourself. Do not say that this is because of me, lest that should be similar to Qārūn who said:

﴿ قَالَ إِنَّمَا أُوتِيتُهُ عَلَىٰ عِلْمٍ عِندِي ﴾

"He said, 'I was only given it because of knowledge I have.'"[al Qaṣaṣ: 78]

Once you truly have faith in this belief you will become someone who takes constant recourse to Allah (عَزَّوَجَلَّ) so that He makes you firm. For certainly:

القلوب بين إِصْبَعَيْن من أَصَابِع الرَّحْمن، كَقَلْبٍ وَاحِدٍ، يصرّفه حيث يشاء

All hearts are like a single heart between two of Allah's fingers. He turns them as He wills.

So all of the slaves hearts are between the Fingers of al-Raḥmān, who turns them as He wills. "If He wills that they deviate, then they deviate and if He wills, He guides them."[25]

However, deviance has a cause, just as Allah (تَبَارَكَ وَتَعَالَىٰ) said:

﴿ فَلَمَّا زَاغُوا أَزَاغَ اللَّهُ قُلُوبَهُمْ ﴾

"And when they deviated, Allah caused their hearts to deviate." [al-Ṣaff: 5]

Once the Prophet (صَلَّى ٱللَّهُ عَلَيْهِ وَسَلَّمَ) conveyed this ḥadīth, he then said:

اللّٰهُمَّ مصرف القلوب صرف قلوبنا على طاعتك

O Allah! Changer of the hearts! Turn our hearts to obeying You!

Be diligent pertaining this heart of yours that is as such that if it is correct, then the entire body will be correct, and if it is

[25] Collected by Muslim (2653) in Kitāb al Qadar, the chapter of Allah's changing the hearts as He wills.

corrupt, then the whole body will be corrupt. O Allah! Correct our hearts! O Allah! Correct our hearts! O Nurturing Lord of the Worlds!

His statement, "*between al-Raḥmān's fingers*" is verified to have come from the Prophet (صَلَّىٰ ٱللَّهُ عَلَيْهِ وَسَلَّمَ). The fact that the heart is between Allah's Fingers does not necessitate that touching or direct contact occurs, lest that it be said that this *ḥadīth* is incorrect because it necessitates that the Fingers of al-Rabb [i.e., the Nurturing Lord] are inside of the chests of human beings. That is because the proponents of *ta'ṭīl* [i.e., negating the literal meanings of divine attributes] negate and reject the meaning of this ḥadīth. They purport that it is not possible. How could the hearts be between the Fingers of al-Raḥmān? In response it is said that something being in-between does not necessitate touching or direct-contact. The proof is Allah's statement (تَبَارَكَ وَتَعَالَىٰ):

﴿ وَالسَّحَابِ الْمُسَخَّرِ بَيْنَ السَّمَاءِ وَالْأَرْضِ ﴾

"And the clouds controlled between the heaven and the earth are signs." [al Baqara: 164].

Do they touch the earth? The answer is no. Do they touch the heaven? The answer is no. Despite that, Allah (عَزَّوَجَلَّ) described that as being in-between. So our hearts being between Allah's Fingers does not necessitate any touching or direct-contact.

If someone were to ask: **how** is it then? The answer is that we respond to him as al Imām Mālik did [to a similar question]: that [the obvious meaning of] "between" is known; the modality [i.e., how it is] is unknown; believing in it is mandatory; and asking about it is a [creedal] innovation. We say something similar to anyone who attempts to ask about the modality of Allah's Attributes, trying to imagine that with his heart. Even if your heart suggests to you to try to search after the modality of Allah's Attributes, then present it with the statement of al Imām Mālik and others from the scholars.

O Allah! Make our hearts firm upon obeying You, O Nurturing Lord of the Worlds!

XII. Concluding Advice

Synopsis of Lines 69-73:

69. Beware of Your Inner-Flaws

70. The Harm of Vindictiveness

71. The Divine Promise of Victory

72. Allah Recompenses People Accordingly

73. Who This Advice is Written For

XII. Concluding Advice (Lines 69-73)

وَاحْذَرْ كَمَائِنَ نَفْسِكَ اللَّاتِي مَتَى ... خَرَجَتْ عَلَيْكَ كُسِرْتَ كَسْرَ مُهَانِ

[69. /(256.)] Be on caution against the innermost facets of your self which are such that if they exited, you'd be broken in degradation.

وَإِذَا انْتَصَرْتَ لَهَا فَأَنْتَ كَمَنْ بَغَى ... طَفْيَ الدُّخَانِ بِمَوْقِدِ النِّيرَانِ

[70. /(257.)] Were you to come to its defense then you would be like one trying to extinguish smoke by lighting a large fire.

وَاللهُ أَخْبَرَ وَهُوَ أَصْدَقُ قَائِلٍ ... أَنْ سَوْفَ يَنْصُرُ عَبْدَهُ بِأَمَانِ

[71. /(258.)] Allah, who is the truest to speak, has informed that He would aid His worshipper with safety.

مَنْ يَعْمَلِ السُّوآى سَيُجْزَى مِثْلَهَا ... أَوْ يَعْمَلِ الحُسْنَى يَفُزْ بِجِنَانِ

[72. /(259.)] Whoever commits heinousness will be recompensed its like; and whoever does what is best will successfully attain Paradise.

هَذِي وَصِيَّةُ نَاصِحٍ وَلِنَفْسِهِ ... وَصَّى وَبَعْدُ لِسَائِرِ الإِخْوَانِ

[73. /(260.)] This is an advice from someone sincere, and it is offered introspectively and then it is issued for all brethren.

Synopsis of Lines 69-73

Muhammad Khalīl Harrās(رَحِمَهُ ٱللَّهُ) summarizes:

Kamā'in is the plural of *kamīna*. The meaning of the self's *kamā'in* (inner-facets) are its bad instincts and base desires. The author is advising that the person be on guard against it [i.e., the self] and to be constantly active in disciplining it whenever it revolts and rebels against him. If he does not, then it will defeat him in a terrible manner that will cause him to be degraded and humiliated thereafter. Just as he must not pursue self-triumphing, then likewise he must cure it and extinguish its revolting. Doing contrary only increases its intensity and its raging. At that point, he would be akin to a person trying to extinguish smoke by igniting a large fire. Rather, it is appropriate that he be patient and forgive, while Allah (عَزَّوَجَلَّ) has promised him victory. He (تَبَارَكَ وَتَعَالَى) informed as much in His Book saying:

﴿إِنَّ اللَّهَ يُدَافِعُ عَنِ الَّذِينَ آمَنُوا﴾

"Indeed, Allah defends those who have believed." [al Ḥajj: 38].

Also, in another verse He (تَبَارَكَ وَتَعَالَى) says:

﴿إِنَّا لَنَنصُرُ رُسُلَنَا وَالَّذِينَ آمَنُوا فِي الْحَيَاةِ الدُّنْيَا وَيَوْمَ يَقُومُ الْأَشْهَادُ﴾

"Verily, We will indeed make victorious Our Messengers and those who believe in this world's life and on the Day when the witnesses will stand forth"[Ghāfir: 51]

Similarly, He has informed that the recompense of an offense is an offense in kind and that the recompense of goodness is Allah's forgiveness and good-pleasure.

69. Beware of Your Inner-Flaws

وَاحْذَرْ كَمَائِنَ نَفْسِكَ اللَّاتِي مَتَى ... خَرَجَتْ عَلَيْكَ كُسِرْتَ كَسْرَ مُهَانِ

[69. /(256.)] Be on caution against the innermost facets of your self which are such that if they exited, you'd be broken in degradation.

'Abd al-Rahmān al-Sa'dī (رَحِمَهُ ٱللَّهُ) explains:

These hidden facets are as such that you can be broken and denigrated by them. Every person contains hidden-facets. Sometimes they surface. If these are overpowered by the efficacy of intelligence and religiosity, then he will be successful; whereas if the former overpowers these two, he will stray and be wretched, unless Allah (عَزَّوَجَلَّ) repairs him by His Mercy.

Sālih al Fawzān (حفظه الله) explains:

Be wary of the evils of your self, for indeed, the most dangerous thing to a person is his self. So long as Allah (عَزَّوَجَلَّ) protects him from the evils of his self, then He will most likely shield him from anything lesser. Accordingly, the Prophet (صَلَّىٱللَّهُعَلَيْهِوَسَلَّمَ) used to say: "We seek Allah's refuge from the evils of our selves and from the bad outcomes of our actions." So once the person is shielded from the evil of his self, then he will most likely be protected from evils beyond it. The danger of the self is enormous. Accordingly, Allah says:

﴿ وَمَن يُوقَ شُحَّ نَفْسِهِ فَأُولَٰئِكَ هُمُ الْمُفْلِحُونَ ﴾

"And whoever is protected from the stinginess of his soul - it is those who will be the successful." [al Ḥashr: 9].

Muhammad bin Sālih al 'Uthaymīn (رَحِمَهُ ٱللَّهُ) explains:

"*Kamā'in*" meaning: that which is hidden and obscure within the self.

﴿ إِنَّ النَّفْسَ لَأَمَّارَةٌ بِالسُّوءِ إِلَّا مَا رَحِمَ رَبِّي ﴾

"Indeed, the soul is a persistent enjoiner of evil, except those upon which my Lord has mercy." [Yusuf: 53]

So he is saying to be cautious of the inner-facets of your self. The soul has inner-facets, meaning things that are veiled, unknown by anyone but Allah (عَزَّوَجَلَّ). It is as al Qaḥṭānī said [in his Nuniyah]:

وَاللهِ لَوْ عَلِمُوا قَبِيحَ سَرِيرَتِي لَأَبَى السَّلَامَ عَلَيَّ مَنْ يَلْقَانِي

"I swear by Allah that if they knew the hideousness of my inward being, that those who encounter me would refuse to greet me with the Salām."

So the human being has inner-facets that only Allah (عَزَّوَجَلَّ) knows. So be on caution against these inner-facets. There are many inner-flaws. It could even be *shirk* with Allah. We ask Allah (عَزَّوَجَلَّ) to grant us well-being. It could be *riyā'* [i.e., doing a deed to be seen favorably by others]. So a person loves to show off and that people see him doing a righteous deed. It could be jealousy of Allah's servants, which is from the traits of the Yahūd. It could be a dislike that Allah's religion should be victorious, or that Allah (عَزَّوَجَلَّ) would make His allies victorious. It could be preferring the temporal world over the hereafter. It could be preferring children and spouses over the hereafter. Allah (تَبَارَكَ وَتَعَالَى) said:

﴿ يَا أَيُّهَا الَّذِينَ آمَنُوا لَا تُلْهِكُمْ أَمْوَالُكُمْ وَلَا أَوْلَادُكُمْ عَن ذِكْرِ اللَّهِ ﴾

"O you who have believed, let not your wealth and your children divert you from remembrance of Allah." [al Munāfiqūn: 9]

It could also be disliking the truth and finding it to be burdensome. It could also be in the form of enmity and hatred toward the believers. There are many more innumerable things that it could be.

What is important is that inner-defects exist, hidden within the heart, requiring purging and cleaning the heart internally and externally. All of us are able to pray with outward reverential humility. A person makes the *takbīr*, raises his hands and places them on his chest. He makes complete *rukū'* and *sujūd*. He recites perfectly. However, the real affair is that of the heart. Is the heart following the limbs — or more accurately — are the limbs following the heart in performing the deed well, or is it just for appearance?

Ibn al Qayyim warned of this issue. May Allah (عَزَّوَجَلَّ) reward him. So be on caution against it and always make your intention to reach Allah (عَزَّوَجَلَّ), for certainly that is the ultimate goal.

Once you have made this the intention, then I swear by Allah (عَزَّوَجَلَّ) that you will forget the temporal world and what it contains. Once you have made your intention to reach Allah (عَزَّوَجَلَّ), to support Allah's religion, and to love and hate for Allah's sake, then you will soon reach the ultimate objective that causes you to forget everything worldly. Rather, you will find blissful living and the good life in this temporal world. However, if your soul pursued this world and its adornments, then you would become exhausted, because this world will never come to you as you wish. But if you wanted Allah (عَزَّوَجَلَّ), then it would come to you as you wish. If you had wanted Allah (عَزَّوَجَلَّ), then it would come to you as you desire.

So be cautious against these inner-facets because if they "*exited out against you, you'd be broken in degradation.*" At this point, the author compares it to a *kamīn* (i.e., an ambush or surprise-attack) in combat. An ambush in combat is that one conceals his location from his enemy and then springs out upon him. When he does that, then he (i.e., the enemy) would be broken.

Look at how *Hawāzin* conducted themselves during the battle of Ṭā'if. They had 3,500 on their side while the Prophet (صَلَّى ٱللَّٰهُ عَلَيْهِ وَسَلَّمَ) and his army consisted of 12,000 persons. So they concealed themselves for ambush in the valley, remaining hidden and obscure. When the Muslims reached the valley, they attacked them. Then whatever transpired occurred except that Allah (عَزَّوَجَلَّ) graciously bestowed His subtle mercy.

So be on caution against the hidden-facets of the soul. Whenever you find any of these hidden-flaws in your heart, then quickly turn to Allah (عَزَّوَجَلَّ). Don't try to produce logical proof (to justify it) and that sort of thing. Instead, turn firstly to Allah (عَزَّوَجَلَّ), because this is what Allah has taught us to do.

﴿ وَإِمَّا يَنزَغَنَّكَ مِنَ الشَّيْطَانِ نَزْغٌ فَاسْتَعِذْ بِاللَّهِ ۚ إِنَّهُ سَمِيعٌ عَلِيمٌ ﴾

"And if an evil whisper comes to you from Shaitan (Satan) then seek refuge with Allah. Verily, He is All-Hearer, All-Knower." [al 'Arāf: 200]

There is no other recourse or salvation besides Allah (عَزَّوَجَلَّ). Do not sit around thinking deeply, trying to ward off these whisperings, because they might overwhelm you. Instead, you are to take recourse to Allah (عَزَّوَجَلَّ) and seek His refuge.

70. The Harm of Vindictiveness

وَإِذَا انْتَصَرْتَ لَهَا فَأَنْتَ كَمَنْ بَغَى ... طَفْيَ الدُّخَانِ بِمَوْقِدِ النِّيرَانِ

[70. /(257.)] Were you to be retributive for its sake, then you would be like one trying to extinguish smoke by lighting a fire.

'Abd al-Rahmān al-Sa'dī (رَحِمَهُ ٱللَّهُ) explains:

Such a person is like one seeking deliverance from hot rocks by leaping into fire.

Sālih al Fawzān (حفظه الله) explains:

He is saying do not seek after personal triumph, but rather seek victory for the truth. As for yourself, then no matter what people trial you with, then be patient with their harm.

Accordingly, the Prophet (ﷺ) was abused and never sought revenge for himself, instead, he only sought victory for Allah's sake. He did not used to become angry for himself. Things were said about him and he was confronted with speech and abuse, yet he never sought out personal victory while he could have defended himself because Allah (عَزَّوَجَلَّ) had given him power and authority. But he never exacted retribution in his own defense. He only pardoned and overlooked while showing good treatment to those who mistreated him. These were his character traits. However, whenever Allah's sanctities were violated, then he would certainly be angry and retributive for Allah's sanctities. So it is imperative upon you to be like that, O believer! Do not seek to prevail for your own sake, but seek to prevail for Allah's sake.

Muhammad bin Sālih al 'Uthaymīn (رَحِمَهُ ٱللَّهُ) explains:

"*Were you to be retributive for its sake*" meaning for yourself. Meaning that you would be a participant in its ambush and would thus be committing a great blunder, like a person who wants to extinguish smoke by igniting a large fire. He wouldn't be able to do so because every ignition would cause more smoke. It would be impossible just like a person trying to extinguish a fire by increasing the firewood.

71. The Divine Promise of Victory

وَاللهُ أَخْبَرَ وَهُوَ أَصْدَقُ قَائِلٍ ... أَنْ سَوْفَ يَنْصُرُ عَبْدَهُ بِأَمَانِ

[71. /(258.)] Allah, who is the truest to speak, has informed that He would aid his worshipper with safety.

Sālih al Fawzān (حفظه الله) explains:

Allah (تَبَارَكَ وَتَعَالَى) said:

﴿ إِنَّا لَنَنصُرُ رُسُلَنَا وَالَّذِينَ آمَنُوا فِي الْحَيَاةِ الدُّنْيَا وَيَوْمَ يَقُومُ الْأَشْهَادُ ﴾

"Verily, We will indeed make victorious Our Messengers and those who believe in this world's life and on the Day when the witnesses will stand forth"[Ghāfir: 51]

He (تَبَارَكَ وَتَعَالَى) also said:

﴿ وَكَانَ حَقًّا عَلَيْنَا نَصْرُ الْمُؤْمِنِينَ ﴾

"And incumbent upon Us was support of the believers.." [al-Rūm: 47]

So long as you do not exact retribution on behalf of yourself, then Allah (عَزَّوَجَلَّ) will aid you, whereas if you exacted personal retribution, then indeed, Allah (عَزَّوَجَلَّ) would leave you alone to deal with your enemy.

Muhammad bin Sālih al 'Uthaymīn (رَحِمَهُ ٱللَّهُ) explains:

Then he said that Allah (عَزَّوَجَلَّ) has informed that He is going to aid his worshipper with safety. The proof for this is His saying (تَبَارَكَ وَتَعَالَىٰ):

﴿ إِنَّا لَنَنصُرُ رُسُلَنَا وَالَّذِينَ آمَنُوا فِي الْحَيَاةِ الدُّنْيَا وَيَوْمَ يَقُومُ الْأَشْهَادُ ﴾

"Verily, We will indeed make victorious Our Messengers and those who believe in this world's life and on the Day when the witnesses will stand forth"[Ghāfir: 51]

Allah (عَزَّوَجَلَّ) proved His promise to be true. Allah (عَزَّوَجَلَّ) aided Muḥammad over his enemies. He had exited from Makkah, fearful and hiding in the cave. He then returned to it [i.e., Mecca] eight years later as a victorious conqueror. For this reason, the Prophet (صَلَّىٰ ٱللَّهُ عَلَيْهِ وَسَلَّمَ) declared during the ritual of *al-sa'ī* (running or brisk walking) between Ṣafā and Marwah:

لَا إِلَهَ إِلَّا اللهُ وَحْدَهُ لَا شَرِيكَ لَهُ، لَهُ الْمُلْكُ وَلَهُ الْحَمْدُ وَهُوَ عَلَى كُلِّ شَيْءٍ قَدِيرٌ، لَا إِلَهَ إِلَا اللهُ وَحْدَهُ، أَنْجَزَ وَعْدَهُ، وَنَصَرَ عَبْدَهُ، وَ هَزَمَ الْأَحْزَابَ وَحْدَهُ،

"Nothing is deserving of worship except for Allah alone without any partner. The dominion and praise are for Him and He has power over all things. Nothing is deserving of worship except Allah (عَزَّوَجَلَّ). He made His promise succeed, He aided His worshipful-servant, and He alone defeated the confederations."

So Allah (عَزَّوَجَلَّ) had informed that He was going to aid His servant and He was truthful. This is what actually happened.

72. Allah Recompenses People According to What They Earn

مَنْ يَعْمَلِ السُّوآى سَيُجزَى مِثْلَهَا ... أَوْ يَعْمَلِ الحُسْنَى يَفُزْ بِجَنَانِ

[72./(259.)] Whoever commits evil will be recompensed its like; and whoever does what is best will successfully attain Paradise.

Muhammad bin Sālih al 'Uthaymīn (رَحِمَهُ ٱللَّهُ) explains:

He also informed that whoever does evil will receive recompense similar to it and that whoever does good will successfully attain Paradise. This is taken from Allah's statement (تَبَارَكَ وَتَعَالَىٰ):

﴿مَّنْ عَمِلَ صَالِحًا فَلِنَفْسِهِۦ ۖ وَمَنْ أَسَآءَ فَعَلَيْهَا ۗ وَمَا رَبُّكَ بِظَلَّٰمٍ لِّلْعَبِيدِ﴾

"Whosoever does righteous good deed it is for (the benefit of) his ownself, and whosoever does evil, it is against his ownself, and your Lord is not at all unjust to (His) slaves." [Fuṣṣilat: 46]

73. Who This Advice is Written For

هَذِي وَصِيَّةُ نَاصِحٍ وِلِنَفْسِهِ ... وَصَّى وَبَعْدُ لِسَائِرِ الإِخْوَانِ

[73./(260.)] This is an advice from someone sincere, and it offered in introspection and then it is for all of his brethren.

Sālih al Fawzān (حفظه الله) explains:

Meaning that he has advised us with these beneficial bits of advice. He began with himself. That is how sincere advisors are. They always begin with themselves and then it is offered to his brothers.

Muhammad bin Sālih al 'Uthaymīn (رحمه الله) explains:

In conclusion: This is the author's advice which he issues introspectively to himself firstly, and then to all of his brothers from those pursuing guidance — the people of genuineness, monotheism, and faith.

Al-Sa'di's Summarization of Ibn al Qayyim's Advice

قال العلامة السعدي في توضيح معاني الكافية الشافية:

في مقدمة نافعة قبل التحكيم:

وَذَلِكَ أَنَّ الْمُؤَلِّفَ جَعَلَ هَذَا الكِتَابَ حُكْمًا وَحَاكِمًا بَيْنَ مَذَاهِبِ الْجَهْمِيَّةِ وَالْمُعَطِّلِينَ وَبَيْنَ مَذَاهِبِ أَهْلِ السُّنَّةِ وَالْجَمَاعَةِ الْمُثْبِتِينَ، وَالحَاكِمُ لَا يُمْكِنُهُ أَنْ يَحْكُمَ بِالْعَدْلِ حَتَّى يَعْلَمَ الْعَدْلَ وَيَتَخَلَّقَ بِالْأَخْلَاقِ الْجَمِيلَةِ وَيَتَخَلَّى عَنِ الْأَخْلَاقِ الرَّذِيلَةِ.

فَأَعْظَمُ الْأَخْلَاقِ الْجَمِيلَةِ الوَاجِبَةِ — خُصُوصًا فِي هَذَا المَقَامِ — هُوَ التَّمَسُّكُ بِكِتَابِ اللهِ وَسُنَّةِ رَسُولِهِ، وَأَنْ يَكُونَ هَذَا الْأَمْرُ هُوَ قَاعِدَةُ الْعَبْدِ وَآخِيَّتُهُ الَّتِي يَرْجِعُ إِلَيْهَا وَيَرُدُّ مَا تَنَازَعَ فِيهِ الْمُتَنَازِعُونَ إِلَيْهِ، فَمَا وَافَقَهُ فَهُوَ الْحَقُّ الْمَقْبُولُ وَمَا نَاقَضَهُ فَهُوَ البَاطِلُ الْمَرْدُودُ، وَمَا لَا يَعْلَمُ مُوَافَقَتَهُ وَلَا مُنَاقَضَتُهُ وَقَفَ فِيهِ حَتَّى يَتَبَيَّنَ أَمْرُهُ.

فَإِذَا بَنَى الْعَبْدُ أَقْوَالَهُ وَعُلُومَهُ وَنَظَرَهُ وَمُنَاظَرَتُهُ عَلَى هَذَا الأَصْلِ أَفْلَحَ وَأَنْجَحَ، وَكَانَ عَلَى ثِقَةٍ مِنْ أَمْرِهِ وَيَقِينٍ مِنْ بَرَاهِينِهِ، وَلَكِنْ لَا يَصْلُحُ هَذَا وَلَا يَتِمُّ إِلَا لِمَنْ كَانَ عَارِفًا بِالْأَدِلَّةِ الشَّرْعِيَّةِ.

وَأَمَا الجَاهِلُ فَمَا يُفْسِدُهُ أَكْثَرُ مِمَّا يُصْلِحُهُ، فَعَلَيْهِ أَنْ يَتَعَلَّمَ لِيَتَكَلَّمَ، فَالجَاهِلُ المُرَكَّبُ الَّذِي لَا يَدْرِي وَلَا يَدْرِي أَنَّهُ لَا يَدْرِي، وَالْجَاهِلُ

الْبَسِيطُ هُوَ الَّذِي لَا يَدْرِي وَيَدْرِي أَنَّهُ لَا يَدْرِي . كِلَاهُمَا إِذَا تَكَلَّمَ كَانَ مَعَ تَحْرِيمِ كَلَامِهِ ضَرَرُهُ أَكْثَرَ مِنْ نَفْعِهِ، سَوَاءٌ انْتَسَبَ إِلَى الْحَقِّ أَوْ إِلَى الْبَاطِلِ.

فَإِذَا وُفِّقَ الْعَبْدُ لِلْعِلْمِ وَرُزِقَ خَشْيَةً للهِ وَإِنْصَافًا بِأَنْ يَكُونَ مُرَادُهُ الْحَقَّ فَيَقْبَلُ الْحَقَّ مَعَ مَنْ كَانَ وَأَيْنَ كَانَ، فَهَذَا مُوَفَّقٌ مَحْمُودٌ. فَإِذَا رُزِقَ مَعَ ذَلِكَ الْإِخْلَاصَ وَالْمُتَابَعَةَ بِأَنْ تَقَعَ أَقْوَالُهُ وَأَفْعَالُهُ وَجَمِيعُ حَرَكَاتِهِ وَسَكَنَاتِهِ خَالِصَةً لِوَجْهِ اللهِ، مُرَادًا بِهَا رِضَاهُ وَطَلَبَ ثَوَابِهِ، وَكَانَ فِي ذَلِكَ دَائِرًا مَعَ سُنَّةِ نَبِيِّهِ فَقَدْ كَمُلَ أَمْرُهُ، وَحِينَئِذٍ لَا يُبَالِي بِكَثْرَةِ الْمُعَارِضِينَ.

وَكُلَّمَا كَثُرَ خُصُومُهُ ازْدَادَتْ شَجَاعَتُهُ لِعِلْمِهِ وَخَشْيَتِهِ وَإِخْلَاصِهِ وَمُتَابَعَتِهِ وَمَعْرِفَتِهِ أَنَّ مَا مَعَهُ مِنَ الْحَقِّ لَا يَثْبُتُ لَهُ الْجِبَالُ الرَّوَاسِي.

فَإِنَّ أَهْلَ الْحَقِّ لَا يُقَاتِلُونَ بِكَثْرَةِ عَدَدٍ وَلَا قُوَّةِ عُدَدٍ مَادِّيَّةٍ، وَإِنَّمَا قُوَّتُهُمْ وَمَدَارُهُمْ عَلَى الْقُوَّةِ الْحَقِيقِيَّةِ الْمَعْنَوِيَّةِ: قُوَّةِ الْإِيمَانِ، وَقُوَّةِ الْحَقِّ وَمَا يَقْتَضِيهِ مِنَ الْمُقَوِّيَاتِ الْمَعْنَوِيَةِ وَمَا يَتْبَعُهَا مِنَ الْقُوَّةِ الْمَادِّيَّةِ، وَبِهَذَا فَتَحَ الصَّحَابَةُ وَالْقُرُونُ الْمُفَضَّلَةُ الْقُلُوبَ بِالْعِلْمِ وَالْإِيمَانِ، وَاحْتَلُّوا بِهَذِهِ الْقُوَّةِ وَبِالْعَدْلِ وَالرَّحْمَةِ الْأَقْطَارَ، لِأَنَّهُمْ جَمَعُوا أَصْنَافَ الشَّجَاعَةِ لِاعْتِمَادِهِمْ عَلَى الْحَقِّ وَزُهْدِهِمْ فِي النُّفُوسِ، وَتَمَامُ ذَلِكَ زُهْدُهُمْ فِي الثَّنَاءِ الْبَاطِلِ، فَإِنَّ هَذِهِ الْأُمُورَ مَتَى اجْتَمَعَتْ تَمَّتِ الشَّجَاعَةُ، وَمَتَى فُقِدَ وَاحِدٌ مِنْهَا أَوْ كُلُّهَا نَقَصَتْ أَوْ فُقِدَتْ .

فَمَنْ لَمْ يَعْتَمِدْ عَلَى الْحَقِّ بَلْ يَنْصُرُ الْبَاطِلَ، فَمَا أَسْرَعَ مَا يُخَالِطُهُ الْجُبْنُ وَالْخَيَالَاتُ الْمُتَوَلِّدَةُ مِنَ الْبَاطِلِ، وَمَنْ لَمْ يَزْهَدْ بِنَفْسِهِ بَلْ حُبِّبَتْ إِلَيْهِ وَلَمْ يَهُنْ عَلَيْهِ إِقْدَامُهَا فِي الْحَقِّ الْمُشِقِّ عَلَى النُّفُوسِ، أَوْ كَانَ يَخْشَى لَوْمَ اللَّائِمِينَ أَوْ يَقِفُ عِنْدَ مَدْحِ الْمَادِحِينَ، أَوْ يُعَرْقِلُ مَسَاعِيَهُ ذَمُّ الذَّامِّينَ، فَهَذِهِ كُلُّهَا عِلَلٌ تُوقِفُ سَيْرَ الْقُوَّةِ وَتَمْنَعُ الشَّجَاعَةَ، فَالْمُحِقُّ الَّذِي لَا يُبَالِي بِالْمَشَاقِّ وَلَا يَقِفُ إِلَّا عِنْدَ مَدْحِ اللهِ وَرَسُولِهِ وَذَمِّهِمَا : هُوَ الْقَوِيُّ الشُّجَاعُ.

وَلَا بُدَّ أَنْ يُبْتَلَى إِذَا وَصَلَ إِلَى هَذِهِ الْحَالِ بِالْمُعْرِضِينَ وَالْمُعَارِضِينَ لَهُ الرَّادِّينَ لِمَا قَالَهُ ، فَإِذَا تَيَقَّنَ أَنَّهُ عَلَى الْحَقِّ وَمَا مَعَ الْمُعَارِضِينَ بَاطِلٌ مَا بَيْنَ بِدْعَةٍ أَوْ فِرْيَةٍ أَوْ رَأْيٍ مُخَالِفٍ لِلشَّرْعِ أَوْ شُبَهٍ وَتَشْكِيكَاتٍ يُشَكِّكُونَ فِيهَا الْخَلْقَ، أَوْجَبَ لَهُ أَنْ يَصْدَعَ بِالْحَقِّ وَلَا يَخْشَى إِلَّا اللهَ .

وَلَكِنَّهُ فِي هَذِهِ الحَالِ يَحْتَاجُ إِلَى صَبْرٍ جَمِيلٍ، وَالْجَمِيلُ مِنْ ذَلِكَ ضِدُّ الْقَبِيحِ، فَهُوَ الخَالِصُ لِوَجْهِ اللهِ، الْمُوَافِقُ لِمَرْضَاةِ اللهِ، الخَالِي مِنْ هَوَى النَّفْسِ وَحَمِيَّةِ الشَّيْطَانِ، وِمِنَ التَّسَخُّطِ وَالشَّكَايَةِ إِلَى الْمَخْلُوقِينَ، بَلْ إِذَا اشْتَكَى فَإِلَى رَبِّ الْعَالَمِينَ، وَيُسْتَعْمَلُ الْهَجْرُ فِي مَحَلِّهِ لِأَهْلِ الْبِدَعِ وَالْإِنْحِرَافِ وَالْمَعَاصِي، حَيْثُ كَانَ فِيهِ مَصْلَحَةٌ وَنَصْرٌ لِلْحَقِّ وَتَخْفِيفٌ لِلْبَاطِلِ وَالشَّرِّ، وَعَلَيْهِ أَنْ يَحْمَدَ اللهَ عَلَى الْهِدَايَةِ إِلَى الْحَقِّ وَيَرْحَمَ الْخَلْقَ، فَإِنَّهُ إِذَا نَظَرَ إِلَى أَقْدَارِ اللهِ إِذْ خَذَلَهُمْ وَوَلَّاهُمْ مَا تَوَلَّوا لِأَنْفُسِهِمْ مِنَ

الْبَاطِلِ وَالْغَيِّ، وَأَبْقَاهُمْ فِي ضَلَالِهِمْ يَعْمَهُونَ، رَحِمَهُمْ وَدَعَا لَهُمْ وَجَدَّ وَحَرَصَ عَلَى السَّعْيِ فِي هِدَايَتِهِمْ بِحَسْبِ إِمْكَانِهِ، ثُمَّ إِذَا نَظَرَ إِلَيْهِمْ بِعَيْنِ الشَّرْعِ وَالْأَمْرِ أَقَامَ عَلَيْهِمْ مَا أَمَرَ بِهِ الشَّارِعُ مِنَ الْعُقُوبَاتِ، وَحَمَلَهُمْ عَلَيْهِ وَعَلَى الْتِزَامِ أَحْكَامِهِ، وَهُوَ مَعَ ذَلِكَ خَائِفٌ مُشْفِقٌ عَلَى إِيمَانِهِ، فَإِنَّ اللهَ مُقَلِّبُ الْقُلُوبِ، فَمَا اسْتُبْقِيَتْ نِعَمُ اللهِ بِمِثْلِ حَمْدِهِ وَالثَّنَاءِ عَلَيْهِ وَالْخَوْفِ وَالْحَذَرِ مِنْ زَوَالِهَا وَالْإِكْثَارِ مِنَ الْإِسْتِعَاذَةِ بِاللهِ مِنْ شَرِّ النَّفْسِ وَسَيِّئِ الْأَعْمَالِ، وَعَلَيْهِ أَنْ يُوَطِّنَ نَفْسَهُ عَلَى الْخُضُوعِ لِلْحَقِّ وَالْإِنْقِيَادِ لَهُ مَعَ مَنْ قَالَهُ، وَسُرْعَةِ الرُّجُوعِ عَنِ الْبَاطِلِ الَّذِي قَالَهُ مُخْطِئًا، وَأَنْ لَا يَعْجَبَ بِنَفْسِهِ وَعَمَلِهِ، وَيَجْعَلَ الرِّيَاسَةَ وَالتَّمَكُّنَ مِنْ قُلُوبِ النَّاسِ مَانِعًا لَهُ مِنْ قَبُولِ الْحَقِّ.

فَإِذَا جَمَعَ اللهُ لِلْعَبْدِ هَذِهِ الْأُمُورَ الَّتِي وَصَّى بِهَا الْمُؤَلِّفُ فِي هَذِهِ الْمُقَدِّمَةِ، وَوَثِقَ بِرَبِّهِ وَتَوَكَّلَ عَلَيْهِ، وَعَلِمَ أَنَّ اللهَ لَا بُدَّ أَنْ يَنْصُرَ الْحَقَّ وَمَنِ اتَّبَعَهُ، نَشِطَتْ نَفْسُهُ وَقَوِيَتْ هِمَّتُهُ وَحَصَلَ عَلَى الْفَلَاحِ وَالنَّجَاحِ، وَاللهُ أَعْلَمُ.

Al 'Allāmah 'Abd al-Raḥmān bin Nāṣir al-Sa'dī (رَحِمَهُ ٱللَّهُ) summarizes Ibn al Qayyim's tremendous advice in his book *Tawḍīḥ al Kāfiyah al-Shāfiyah.* He wrote:

> One cannot justly arbitrate until first being knowledgeable of justice and incorporating beautiful character traits — while ridding himself of loathsome characteristics.
>
> The most mandatory of beautiful character traits, specifically in this instance, is holding fast to Allah's book and His Messenger's Sunnah. Furthermore, this matter must be the slave's guiding principle and companion, constituting his point of reference to which he refers differing parties. Whatever conforms to it is the conceded truth and whatever contradicts it is rejected falsehood. When he is unknowing of whether or not something conforms to it or contradicts it, then he withholds from rendering judgment until the matter is clear.
>
> So when a person bases their statements, knowledge, investigating, and debating upon this foundation, then he will succeed and attain accomplishment. He will be have the wherewithal to have confidence about his situation and have certainty about his evidences. However, this will not be adequate or complete for any person save he who is intimately aware of religious evidence. As for an ignoramus, then he will ruin more than he rectifies, so it is upon him to learn so that he might then speak. The person of compound ignorance, who does not know that he does not know, and the person of basic ignorance, who knows that he does not

know — when either speak, despite it being forbidden for him to do so, then their harm is greater than their benefit. This is the same whether they ascribe to the truth or to falsehood.

When a person is guided to knowledge and is endowed with fear of Allah (عَزَّوَجَلَّ) as well as objectiveness so that the truth is his purpose — accepting the truth regardless of who and where it is found — then such a person is truly guided and praiseworthy. Alongside all of that, once he is endowed with sincerity and following the Sunnah: such that his statement, deeds, activity, and inactivity is sincere engaged in for Allah's face, thereby seeking His good-pleasure and pursuing His reward; while operating within the sphere of the Sunnah of His Prophet (صَلَّىٱللَّهُعَلَيْهِوَسَلَّمَ) — then his situation will be complete. At such a point he will not care about the quantity of those who disagree.

The more his opponents increase, the more courageous he will become on account of: (1) his knowledge; (2) his fear (of Allah (عَزَّوَجَلَّ)); (3) his sincerity; (4) his following the Sunnah; and (5) his intimate awareness of the fact that the tallest mountains could not stand their ground against what he has of the truth.

The people of truth do not fight in terms of quantity of numbers or material support. Rather, their strength and striking position is built upon true spiritual strength, the power of faith, the power of truth, and what that dictates of incorporeal reinforcements and what resultantly follows of material strength.

By way of this, the *Ṣaḥāba* (رَضِيَ ٱللَّهُ عَنْهُمْ) and the best generations of this nation conquered the hearts with knowledge and faith, while occupying territories with this strength, accompanied by justice and mercy. This is because they mobilized the components of courage by way of their dependence upon the truth and disinterest in the self (i.e. selflessness). From the totality of that was their disinterest in false praise. Certainly, whenever these matters are assembled, courage comes into full fruition, whereas, if one or all of these matters were to be absent, it would be absent or deficient.

As for he who does not rely on the truth, but rather defends falsehood, then how swiftly does he become confused by cowardice and delusions that are spawned out of falsehood. When one does not render oneself selfless, but, instead, is in love with the self, therefore not finding it to be something insignificant to advance for the sake of the truth — which is already difficult upon the self: whoever fears the blame of the blamers, stops once receiving praise, or whose endeavor is impeded by the dispraise of critics — then all of these matters are defects that stop the flow of strength and prevent courage.

The genuine person is one who does not care about hardships and only takes pause to consider what Allah (عَزَّوَجَلَّ) and the Messenger (صَلَّىٱللَّهُعَلَيْهِوَسَلَّمَ) have praised or dispraised: such are the strong and the brave. Once a person arrives at this condition, he will inexorably be tried with those that show aversion and disagree, refuting what he says. Once he is certain that he is upon the truth and that what his opponents have is false: ranging in-between religious innovation, slander, opinions running contrary to the religion, confusion, or doubts employed to confound the people — then this mandates for him to unflinchingly advance the truth, fearing nothing but Allah (عَزَّوَجَلَّ).

However, in this state, he is in need of beautiful patience and beautiful clemency. The beautiful variation of this is the opposite of its unattractive form. It is that which is: carried out sincerely for Allah's face; conforming to what pleases Allah (عَزَّوَجَلَّ); void of selfish impulse and of Satanic inspired defensiveness; and it is free from being upset and complaining to the creation. Rather, if he complains, then he would do so to Rabbil 'Ālamīn. He also employs ostracizing in its proper place — as relates people of religious innovation, deviation, and sinfulness — when that entails benefit, aiding the truth, and diminishing falsehood and evil.

Furthermore, it is upon him to praise Allah (عَزَّوَجَلَّ) for guiding him to the truth while having mercy towards the creation. For certainly, when he looks at what Allah (عَزَّوَجَلَّ) destined in forsaking them, entrusting them to what they aligned themselves with of falsehood and deviance, and his leaving them to stumble in their misguidance: he pities them, prays for them, strives, and diligently endeavors in guiding them according to his ability.

Furthermore, when looking at them with the eye of the religion and divine commandment, then he establishes what Allah (عَزَّوَجَلَّ) has ordered of punitive measures. He hoists them onto it and to adherence of its laws. While doing so, he is fearful and afraid for his own *emān*, for certainly Allah (عَزَّوَجَلَّ) is the changer of hearts. Nothing retains Allah's blessings like: (1.) praising and extolling Him; (2.) being fearful and cautionary of their disappearance, (3.) striving to take the means that facilitate them, (4.) avoiding what eradicates [blessings] such as oppositional behavior, conceitedness and despotism; (5.) and seeking Allah's refuge from the evil of the self and the unfavorable outcomes of actions.

It is upon the person to: train himself to by humble and submit to the truth despite who states it; to quickly recant from falsehood he mistakenly says; to not be amazed with oneself or actions; and not to allow any sort of leadership or status that he has achieved in people's hearts to be an obstacle from accepting the truth.

Once Allah (عَزَّوَجَلَّ) combines these matters —which the author advised with in this introduction — within one of His slaves, whereupon he trusts and relies on Allah, (عَزَّوَجَلَّ) knowing that Allah (عَزَّوَجَلَّ) will definitely aid the truth and its followers, then his self will be energized, his ambition strengthened, and he will attain success and accomplishment.

Printed in Great Britain
by Amazon

20030388R00140